Acclaim for

Sometime, Idaho

"Bartholdt's words are wholly formed and perfect, his tales ring true, they are full of affirmation and understanding of the out-of-doors, and entirely in touch with the rhythms of not just North Idahoan, but human life."

—Tony McDermott
(Former Idaho Fish and Game Commissioner)

"Reading Ralph Bartholdt is like taking a trip through the dusty back roads of the Inland Northwest and stopping at its fishing holes and hunting camps, general stores and bars, to meet salt-of-the-earth locals, people whose tales might never have reached the outside world if not for his insightful eye and pen."

—Andy Walgamott, *Northwest Sportsman Magazine*

"In these short essays, Bartholdt takes us into the wild and sometimes surreal world of fishing and hunting, of mountains and sunsets, hooks, bullets and backroads, where the view often amazes and always entertains..."

—Tim Trainor, *The East Oregonian*

short essays by

RALPH BARTHOLDT

Sometime, Idaho

Ralph Bartholdt's writing and photography have appeared nationally and in regional publications throughout the Pacific Northwest. As a reporter he has worked for news organizations in Washington, Montana and Idaho, Western Europe and as an embedded photojournalist with the 1st Marines in Iraq's Anbar Province. His work has been recognized by the Idaho Press Club, National Newspaper Association, the Associated Press and the Society of Professional Journalists. He lives and writes from Idaho's Panhandle.

Sometime, Idaho

RALPH BARTHOLDT

Sometime, Idaho

ESSAYS

GRASSY MOUNTAIN PRESS

St. Maries, Idaho

ISBN: 978-0-578-59511-5 (Paperback)

Library of Congress Control Number: 2019916359

Portions of this book are works of nonfiction. Some of these essays
have appeared in *Northwest Sportsman* magazine, *The St. Maries
Gazette Record*, *Skookumfoto.blogspot.com*, *The Lewiston Tribune*
and the *Coeur d'Alene Press*.

Photos by Ralph Bartholdt.
Book design by Benjamin Riley.

Printed by kdp.amazon.com

First printing edition 2019.

skookumfoto.blogspot.com

for Helga Wenk

Contents

Autumn

Winter

Spring

Summer

Autumn

SOMETIME, IDAHO

Pheasants And Fair Chase

By the time we reached the wheat fields, the dog had already thrown up once and was looking at me from his place on the passenger side floor boards, fangs of saliva dripping off his jowls, his eyes dour, pleading to please just stop.

The windshield wipers weren't keeping up with the rain and wind gusts bowed the trees on the side of the highway, stripping them of leaves. The summer slick wheels of our car skated back and forth between the lines. It wasn't yet daylight, at least not by the book, and the boy was sleeping in the back seat.

I was focused on drinking coffee, keeping the car keeled downstream and the dog from upchucking into the side door compartment.

No, buddy, I coaxed. Easy now.

The three of us were on our way to kill some birds and Idaho's Palouse wheat fields, rising from the dawn, were the stubble dreams that kept this notion together.

I like telling my kids about the time back in the day when I regularly destroyed 23 of 25 clays on the trap range. Those difficult shots afield seem more prevalent now than the many pheasants, grouse and assorted wildfowl that winged idly away unscathed as the wad of my shot shell petered skyward. Introspection however reminds me of one pheasant in particular that busted downhill straight away as I unloaded a Mossberg 12, the bird disappearing untouched into the last evening of a season long ago.

These are No. 6 shells, I told the boy that morning as we loaded up in the pitch black monsoon, not those No. 8 low base that we use on grouse. He knew. Blearily he recited to me the definition memorized, or something close to it, from his hunter safety training manual as he tumbled into the backseat, asleep before we left the driveway.

When much later we parked along a gravel road in another county in the gray early morning light, the dog realizing his journey on the Santa Maria had passed, perked up. Empty stomach, sharp-eyed, with a muzzle coated with lint, he pointed at a group of cows in a nearby field and made them uneasy. This bolstered his confidence.

The wind had lessened now and the rain was a drizzle.

I woke the boy who wiped the sand from his eyes, ate a bite-size Snickers, and sniffed some coffee before we crawled under a barbed-wire fence and into the tall grass of a lowland meadow. Ten minutes later the first rooster cackled skyward.

Ring-necked pheasants, known as China hens in the old literature, are, like chukar, an Asian import. Introduced to the western U.S. in the late 1800s, the birds flourished in Washington and Oregon before being established in the Midwest — a land that likes to lay claim to the longtails.

We didn't claim the first rooster. Or, the second.

They squawked, clucked and fluttered into the air and didn't come down. Not for a couple hundred yards despite our best efforts.

Hours of preparation hadn't helped. During my son's introduction to clay pigeons weeks earlier, he dusted many with his youth 20-gauge, and twice shot a double.

Out here it was different.

What happened? I asked.

I panicked, he said.

It went like this for most of the morning.

Seven birds up, one bird down.

In one scenario, a pheasant trio, spooked from the edge of a high field, glided into a patch of swamp grass 100 yards away. We hatched a plan, the boy, the dog and I. Sniggering at the prospect of shooting ducks in a barrel, we snuck toward the place where the ringnecks had landed. Like overweight cats loaded down with our guns and shells and game bags, we were slow, but sure-footed and purring. Except for the dog who eyed us with rancor.

What followed was a vaudeville skit, very loud, with nothing coming down but the curtain.

My son hung his head.

"It's called hunting, not killing," I said, in a voice like Father Knows Best. "You're learning a lot about hunting today."

The only thing missing was the Borkum Riff.

Four hours later, one bird down and back in the car, we talked about the hunt as hunters are prone to. Reliving the pieces, the missed shots and the one that connected. Pup and the cows made a pact of mutual respect before I set the dog on the passenger side floor boards and we headed north.

Leaving, however, required a small task asked of us as hunters using land that others worked and fenced and made a living from. I filled out a survey at a box next to the road. Idaho Department of Fish and Game Access Yes! surveys help the department know whether or not it's worth spending our money renting a good piece of ground for the public to enjoy, where people can take their children to pass forward the hunting tradition, and maybe get a bird or two in the process. This is land where city-reared pups can learn to point and retrieve and how a cow on the hoof deserves respect too.

So that's what I did.

I only wrote one word.

Fantastic! I said.

Night Falls On Boggan's Oasis

People all over know more about Boggan's Oasis than I do. I was there a couple of times, mostly to admire Eastern Oregon's Grand Ronde River, which flows into the Snake between steep canyons that bloom in spring, but remain mostly brown dry in other seasons.

I did not venture to wet a line upstream of Boggan's near Troy, Oregon, where a friend stayed one season to fish steelhead without me, and I didn't venture downstream where the Schumaker Road sputters to a conclusion with a canyon wall sporting a few sprigs of greenery in arid rifts above the river.

For a lot of people who traveled Highway 129 between Enterprise, Oregon and Asotin, Washington, just an hour south of Lewiston, Idaho, without the accoutrements of a fishing life, Boggan's was a mix of hostelry, nostalgia and good eats.

For others, it was a place to glean fishing advice, tips, a

handful of plugs, flies and some spare line or leader while chasing steelhead that pressed into the river after spending a year or two in the Pacific Ocean on the other side of the state.

Although Boggan's burned to the ground more than a year ago, its small rental cabins remain a haven for overnighters, or adventurers who linger longer.

Before it disappeared in a puff of late-night smoke, the decor in Boggan's cafe recalled the 1970s, and its heaping servings, shakes, pie and ice cream were served deliciously often by the owners Bill and Farrel Vail.

The Vails are in their 80s and when Boggan's, the business they ran for more than 30 years, burned to the ground on a crisp November night as they watched a Gonzaga basketball game on TV in their nearby home, they pledged to reporters they wouldn't rebuild.

They put the business behind them.

They will miss the patrons they said.

Not the long hours.

They will miss the seasons.

And we will miss Boggan's

The cabins are still available to rent, however, and the RV spaces remain, but a lot of what Boggan's was for its many visitors, is now relegated to memory.

Every state has a Boggan's.

Every out-of-the-way canyon or dirt road that leads to adventure and memories of times less frequented by modern conveniences has a Boggan's. They are the last ditch stops where a traveler can get gas and a T-shirt. They are characteristic and cling to memory, and if memory fails, they show up decades later in photographs yellowed, or on a postcard.

By that time, tragically, they may be gone for good and referenced only in conversation.

They are relegated to history then, and it's just as well.

Once they are gone they cannot be replaced and photographs, no matter their value as a documentary depiction, do them little justice. Aroma, vernacular and that one-particular steelhead rig don't lend themselves to postcards.

Tucked into a deep canyon directly alongside an out-of-the-way river, Boggan's was named for its founder, who in the 1940s built at the only highway crossing of the Grand Ronde River where sea-run rainbows moved with pyrexic determination.

Travelers heading between Lewiston and La Grande or Pendleton, Oregon have two steep and winding grades to traverse with patience and one foot near the brake. Knowing Boggan's was at the bottom of both turned the trip's quiet misery to one of buoyant anticipation.

What's left since the fire has deformed metal and left a hole in the air where decades there was none, is a caved-in roof and gutted windows like eye sockets in the carcass of a spawned salmon. The memories regardless of how we deem them will stick around long after the smoke is washed away.

Northwest Sportsman magazine editor Andy Walgamott spent a couple weeks one spring 20 years ago using Boggan's as a steelheader's base camp.

"I remember back in '99, after the day's steelheading was done, eating dinner there and tracking the Zags as they made their first deep run in the Final Four," Walgamott wrote on his magazine's Facebook page. "I remember the kindness and wonderful meals served up by the owners."

After Boggan's burned, unbelievers drove great distances to ascertain if the rumors were true. It has always been here, and is unlikely that it is no longer, they seemed to tell themselves as they idled near, parking in the lot once full with cars and pickup trucks. They got out of their rigs and walked around.

In the end, they all in their own way bid adieu to one of their favorite wayside haunts.

Max Wilson told a Lewiston Tribune reporter he ate burgers at Boggan's as a boy in the 1940s and '50s, and built the cabinets and the ice cream counter for the restaurant decades later.

Cindi Hill of LaGrande told the newspaper, "This is everybody's stop that comes and goes. A lot of people are gonna miss this place."

In a quickly changing world of tetra bytes and cloud storage, self driving cars, face detection devices and 360-degree selfies, knowing Boggan's existed at all — at the bottom of a notorious canyon near the best steelheading in a small, arid and mostly silent part of the world — was a kind of mental oasis.

It soothed the mind to know Boggan's was there year after

year without a lot of change.

It still soothes the mind to know it was there.

So, that hasn't changed.

Except Boggan's is gone.

SOMETIME, IDAHO

Hunting Dogs Make Emotions Run The Gamut

It wasn't my intention to talk about dogs again, but when Nancy came home after walking The Beast, the topic of our German shorthair's lack of social graces stuck in my mind like a face plant.

Nancy was resigned to the ugliness of our dog's behavior in human company.

"Ill-mannered," she said. "Jumping up on people."

Add it to the incessant high-tailing, as high as a docked tail will go, during field work and the dog's inherent sassiness, which was evident when we perused the litter a couple years ago and chose "growly" because of his spunk.

What sealed the deal on the pup was the breeder's highly valued two cents.

"That's my favorite one," the breeder said, so we thought luck was with us, and we gave each other the "Nanu Nanu" sign.

In my mind, we're lucky still, because during hunts The Beast locks on birds like a radar-guided missile set on seek and destroy.

A lot of dogs don't.

Despite his lack of manners at baseball games, inside the fence of play parks and during leash walks around the pet-populated neighborhoods where we live, The Beast does exactly what his gene code demands.

He is a bird-seeking machine.

The rest is up to us, I suppose.

And that is why we do not feed him a gallon of buttermilk and a pound of hamburger in one sitting.

We could, mind you, but we know our gentle rearing of this tick-marked tongue-hanger sometimes leads to mishaps that lead to anger and a sort of tribulation only other owners of ill-mannered bird hounds understand. So, we cut out the trifecta of ground beef and buttermilk, and a post-meal doggie nap on the warm kitchen floor by the heat vents.

We have decided this fairly recently.

More specifically we adopted this rule last week, prompted by the story of another shorthair owner who described in detail the time "I almost shot my dog."

This erudite and well-spoken hidalgo of the field admitted to filling, at times, once he got ticked, his dog's butt with lead for ranging too far after quail and other upland game subject to gentlemanly pursuits.

But it was his own good intentions that once almost had this squire cross the line where one becomes a Wile E. Coyote or a Yosemite Sam in pursuit of the animated violence of retribution.

His pointer had worked miracles that day in the field,

maintaining gracefully long casts and tight points and bringing harvested birds to hand without hesitation. As a reward, the hunter, accompanied by his new bride, stopped at the store on the way home from the hunt to a house recently purchased.

He wanted a gallon of buttermilk and a pound of burger as a treat for the dog.

"But she talked me out of it," he recalls these years later.

At his new bride's insistence, he purchased a quart of buttermilk instead with the pile of burger and fed it to the pointer with a smile and watched the dog gorge himself until he looked like the inflated drum of a skin boat.

You could have played Merry Melodies with a spoon on his belly.

The dog hunkered down in the kitchen and soon, fast asleep, dreamed of his exploits while whimpering, sleep-running and passing gas before the inevitable happened.

It happened all over the new floor like Texas crude from a just-tapped oil well, and the dog slept on until the hunter and his bride took notice.

This was a malodorous gusher and there was little recourse.

But, you see, here's the rub:

Even after (give it a day) such a violent and unintentional intestinal storm, there is fondness.

Even after the bad behavior. The yapping and licking, and digging in the yard. Even after stealing food from people's plates and the leg-lifting in places where etiquette is required, even then.

It's forgiven, because.

Sometimes a blessing is standing in a field and watching for an hour or more as a pointer works the air and the ground, back and forth like a scythe or a swift and incongruous fan blade made of muscle and bone, ears and a nose.

A tight point and the patience to wait as the hunter approaches within range is a miracle too.

And not even a crude spill on a newlywed's fresh kitchen floor will overshadow it.

It is the untamed miracle of the double helix made perfect in a quiet field away from the casual distortions and the white noise of fast-walking humanity that we see in a pointer.

And why we love these dogs so.

Worms, Foil-Wrapped Grub And Insight

Les at the Rose Lake Conoco wasn't surprised.

He had pondered, as Les sometimes does during his work day chatting with customers, stocking shelves, filling coffee canisters ("That one on the left should be full ... the far left.") whether early season hunters would find birds in their usual early season haunts.

I had just told Les that I walked three miles of brushy road in a place usually good for ruffed grouse on September mornings, but this morning was a bust.

"I was wondering about that," Les said. "It's been so dry."

And it had. The spring was wet and there was a lot of snow to melt from a winter that was mournfully damp if that adequately describes snow to the window frames, but it heated up quickly and June came in blazing followed by a July of heat waves that kindled the forest floor, caused the moss in many places to crunch under foot and curled the leaves of the chokecherry bushes, viburnum and other grouse foods.

Les, who grew up in St. Maries and whose dad in retirement tinkered a lot and flew an airplane, has been grounded in the gas station and convenience store business for decades, but before then, as a kid, he was wildly enthusiastic as anyone about carrying a scattergun into the woods for birds, or hunkering along a field edge to watch antlered deer emerge to nibble on clover.

When he bought the gas station after college he made it a place where loggers stopped for a cheeseburger after work and to chat, where logging truck drivers found hospice and a wonderful variety of heated hand food, and he widened the parking space and opened the doors at 5 a.m. to accommodate retirees and their diesel pickup trucks.

He knew what the general populace who spent a lot of time behind the steering wheel wanted when they stopped for fuel.

In the chunk of years, back in the day, as they say, in which I spent an inordinate amount of time driving in search of places to cast for trout on the west slope of the Rockies I found Les' coffee canisters always full, and the Java in them invariably hot and delicious.

This is an unusual diversion from most roadside gas and grub joints where the coffee tastes as if it's poured from an ashtray and the clerks don't care. And it is why Les has a few chairs set up along a wall, so people can sit a spell and enjoy a cup of Joe.

It wasn't the coffee that had my kids calling Les' place by its accoutrements.

Over the years they referred to Les' store as, "the worm

store," because of the bait that Les sold, which the kids used to cast from the docks to lure Rose Lake bluegills. It was also, "the breakfast store," for the paper-wrapped meals of sausage, bacon, ham and eggs bought from Les' version of a hot case — a stand-up shelf in which to better eye the steaming, freshly hot wares, and "the popcorn place" because Les kept on hand a freshly popped batch made from a commercial popper like at the movies.

We bought the crunchy, burrito-type meals that the kids liked in twos, because it was necessary. One at a time wouldn't cut it.

The kids, road-bleary and blanket-wrapped on our way to a river woke only long enough to peel back the greasy paper and inhale the pork and egg fests one at a time before retiring to ticker tape dreams — from early morning sun flickering through passing trees and the car's window — you only get on the road.

Foremost, we also referred to Les' place as the "cheeseburger store" for its hot, foil-wrapped palate busters.

"We better get to the cheeseburger store before the log truck drivers get there," the kids would mumble knowing they weren't the only ones whose road-induced appetites hungered for one of Les' foil-tucked, cheesy beefsteaks.

For the everyday outdoor enthusiasts, however, Les offers more than the photographs of dead big game animals pinned to the cork board by the door.

He offers insight gleaned from members of the early-morning coffee crew that lounge for a spell on the steel, foam-backed chairs as they sip brew from Styrofoam cups and ponder politics, timber, grain and gas prices and how the duck, or whitetail season might pan out before heading to work.

And he's spent his years watching the management of North Idaho fish and game.

His observations and questions have spurred articles, and served as a gauge of opinion and insight.

"I haven't seen a lot," Les might say regarding dead elk in the back of pickup trucks during the rifle season.

"No one is really talking about it," he might muse about a topic's significance.

Or, "I've wondered if ..."

Which usually starts something.

The inside of his store, located at the junction of the Coeur d'Alenes and the road to the St. Joe is innocuous. There aren't a bunch of dead heads on the walls peering at customers through glass eyes, but there is one particular mounted bass that a mutual friend asked Les to hold on to while he traveled, and for years he traveled a lot.

It is a big enough bass, and wild looking, taken at Rose Lake proper, which lies just a few miles away. It hangs on an archway overlooking the coffee pots, its tail appears to smash spray that conceivably should shower the store with a burst of lake water.

The bass probably gets people to thinking, quietly to themselves, that maybe fishing is a better way to spend the day as opposed to whatever they have listed to do.

Last Monday was just another day at the store for Les.

"I'm here every Monday," he said.

Laboring as he has for decades.

Grounded and pondering grouse.

"Just because the grouse aren't there today, doesn't mean they won't be there tomorrow," Les might say, if you stop by to ask him.

And as usual, Les would be right.

He has time to think. And the patience to make his thoughts count.

SOMETIME, IDAHO

Unnatural Landscapes Are Natural Places For Game

We hunted the railroad rights of way mostly for hare, ruffed grouse and the occasional pheasant that tucked itself into the brambles and sumac, and then flushed cackling with all the color of autumn.

As youngsters, sometimes with guns too big for a grow-in fit, we let loose as piously as pushing the bow on a violin.

The shots rolled out, and the shells ejected in a symphony of ear-bending percussion — and powder burns, however inconsequential, on tender hands and arms.

Red and green shell casings flipped into the air and the bouquet of burned cordite rippled around us as gently as perfume behind the counter at Macy's, minus the lipstick.

If the bird didn't fold like a sweet, September postal package that the dogs rushed out to retrieve, it kept going, flapping its wings and vexing us with its rancorous clucking.

A couple distant cackles, short and to the point, drifted toward us as the pheasant disappeared into the distance on wings pumping then gliding, as it sought a hideaway more quiet and secure without boys, dogs and hand-me-down guns.

Because of birds, railroad rights-of-way were boss.

Once at Harrison, I stood on the tracks of the Union Pacific and flushed three grouse from the railroad brush that were gulped one at a time by the setting sun.

A yellow dog looked at me forlornly and then at least pretended to look for the birds that I had shot toward, but missed.

They weren't there.

My swing was off, and besides, they had scared the heck out of me as they tumbled into the aspens of the former Springston mill site.

The railroad tracks aren't there either, anymore, but the railroad mound survives as a bicycle trail and state park. Its right-of-way extends out to 300 feet in places that are off limits to gunning for birds.

In most places where we live these days, the land is changed and the unnatural changes — railroad grades, roads reclaimed by trees, planted orchards whose homesteaders are long gone having packed up everything but the trees, and clearcuts, those places where the trees are taken — are often where we find the birds, deer and elk we're after.

Rip rap is another such place.

A fishing guide who once tested my sanctimony by asking what I thought of the big boulders placed by backhoes to keep river banks in check, gleefully responded to my approval of them with the words, "They sure do fish!"

And they serve better than the old Nash Super 600s, Pontiac Chieftains or 1947 Super Deluxe Sedans that line the banks of some streams in the West. Granted, there have been sizeable rainbows caught in the vicinity of submerged, riparian car bumpers.

The guide had us fish the bubble line along stretches of rip rap that fell from farm fields into the river; shards of white granite as big as recliners that predictably held fish. Brown trout and rainbows hammered the streamers, or the nymph and dry fly combinations we tossed at them.

The most impressive feat was watching this guide, a kid from New York who was fishing his way to Alaska one river at a time, tie a blood knot with two hands on the oars and the line in his teeth while bouncing through rapids.

I have not mastered the skill.

A friend who guided us on a hairy part of a home river was intent on duplicating the trick at the cost of his attention span.

His hands left the oars, and we careened into a sweeper, a dead tree fallen across the river just high enough to knock everyone from the boat. We all ducked and stayed dry, but paid with a $300 fly rod that broke in three places, and $100 fly line that finally did too.

I still have the rod's cork and the reel.

In hindsight, the slow moving water along the rip rap would have fished a lot better.

SOMETIME, IDAHO

Uncle Jim At The Crossroads

My uncle Jim was 84 when he killed a buck on the first morning of whitetail deer season.

This isn't an easy accomplishment in the brushy, rocky, pastureless swamp country that Jim called home.

He often rode what he called a mini bike out to his hunting grounds along a black top road as narrow as a pinstripe, and ditched the small motorcycle in a bunch of aspens along a dirt logging spur. He climbed the angled ground that rose to a hogsback before falling off into a tamarack swamp of many square miles that trickled north like a spongy and vast carpet of saber-like snags and towering green treetops.

This is where, over a period of many years, he had hung a series of tree stands — the use of them depending on wind and when the last deer had ambled through, browsing on dry grapes, catkins, elderberries or the grasses at the swamp's edge.

He placed a strand of steel tie-wire over trails like gates.

The deer bumped them and pushed past, leaving them open without knowing it. The open gates signaled the deer's direction of travel and Jim quietly pointed this out to hunting pals as they stood nearby, their cheeks reddened from the hike through the swamp wearing heavy woolen jackets, trousers and LL Bean lace up boots.

"Looks like they came through heading west," he might say, his white breath climbing through the tangle of aspen, balsam fir and birch into the November morning like an ice chest opening and closing. "That means they will come back using the north trail."

And he would hike to that place on a rocky finger over a trail of moss and lichen, and climb up into a wooden deer stand nailed to a couple poplars where he waited for the deer to pass. He often spent the day waiting until he shivered and his jaws rattled and it grew dark. He took into account the wolves that cycled through every couple weeks — and when the wolves came, he moved to another area, returning when he figured they had passed on their more or less circular, two-week route through his north country hunting grounds.

When he was 84, he telephoned me.

He had killed a 5-by-5, dragged it from the woods, quartered it and hung the meat from the rafters in his garage along the lake before noon on opening day.

"Let's hope you can do that when you're 84, Ralphie" he extolled.

That's how he referred to me since I was 2, so I took no offense. I still think of it.

The feat.

Much of the time.

Especially when hunting season yawns cold and dark and I test joints in general as well as my own willingness to slip into the black, ice-sharp morning to a far-off trail to ambush elk or deer at first shooting light.

It takes mettle and anyone who disputes it ought to give it a try for a season, if only to gauge temperament.

It's easier with youth, and a hunting pal to keep you on track, but Jim in his later years had neither and seemed to prefer it like that.

So when I hear of hunters filling their tags at first light on opening day I don't call it luck, unless we agree luck is preparation meeting opportunity.

There are other words for it, like heart, determination, focus, and in the case of Jim, sweetness.

Because hope at any age is sweet. And I have years to tend the hope to duplicate Jim's feat.

The buck he said he killed with a running shot from a lever action .30-30 as it leapt through the brush became his last — and likely his sweetest — hunting adventure.

It was an opportunity Jim met with grit and a good shooting eye.

As well as the sweetness of being prepared.

SOMETIME, IDAHO

They Shoot Urban Bucks, Don't They?

The deer head came along with the luggage, the boxes of books, bedding, firearms and the cat, a gray mousy looking feline that feared the sight of most humans but slept on my pal's pillow and in his laundry baskets.

The deer head was from a big, solid antlered, 4x4 whitetail buck, mounted in classic fashion like the ones that stared across rooms from their perch over the mirror in taverns from Penobscot to the outer fringes of Portland during what I call the great modern American hunting epoch, which is really no more than a few decades spanning from the mid 1960s to the early 2000s. After that, hunting became a sort of fringe sport practiced by people who weren't afraid to drag a knife over a whetstone, shun the ever ubiquitous coffee drink and talk openly about their lust for red meat. Idaho became a fringe state for fringe hunters who were really outcasts from the increasingly urbane environs creeping inland from both coasts.

This deer head, however, one could say without sacrificing

fidelity, was a pride piece for my pal who pinned it to the many livingrooms he shared often with others, and then finally with a woman of his choosing.

She didn't like the head despite having grown up around hunters and their prizes, or maybe because of it, and it found a place in a garage, and then a box, in a closet, until the couple split.

The head then sprang forth with vigor and new life, over a ratty couch in a downtown apartment in Montana a few two-steps from several taverns with similar glassy eyed replicas of once vibrant big game. My friend's deer head however — stalwart and hinting at the hunt in a far-off backwood where it was finally slain — looked older and more astute. The white on its muzzle seemed to have spread since I first saw it 15 years earlier, although I could not be certain.

It was in one of the taverns known as a place where writers sit on high stools to better look each other in the eye as they lie about their fishing and hunting exploits, a couple cross walks from my pal's apartment, that he came clean.

He had shot the heavy and symmetrically-antlered 4x4 out of an apple tree in the backyard of his parent's house using a walkie talkie to communicate with his dad who was inside peeking from a window by the porch light. When my friend signaled, his dad flipped the switch and my pal pulled the trigger on a crossbow real quiet like, harvesting the wild, chrysanthemum-fed buck from a distance of 16 feet well before legal shooting light and without waking the neighbors.

The deer had been poached in a backyard in town between

the swingset and the hot tub deck.

So, there you have it.

This isn't an uncommon phenomenon.

In neighborhoods across this great nation men and women far better than I become infatuated during the equinox with the synergy of calcium, diurnal rhythms and testosterone.

Antlers drive people dopey.

So they scheme how best to muster a live set without all that, you know, tough guy stuff, like getting up early, gulping coffee without cream, traipsing into the scary night where coyotes snarl and big cats lurk, and without having to shiver in the frost like a shih tzu in an ice box, and then testing the outermost limits of their patience as they wait, wait, wait — and maybe come up short.

Odds are against killing big bucks, or any buck for that matter.

So the easy route, the one that fate portends, and comfort demands, becomes the most doable.

I don't decry the harvesting of city deer. It's legal in some places, or at least, as a deputy explained, not against the law as written in county statutes.

Urban whitetails are, afterall, more akin to rodents of a questionable gene pool while their cousins high up in the hills tend the genuine double helix.

So what the heck?

It seems cheesy though, doesn't it, to stalk city deer before shooting light as they nibble rhododendron planted by the department of parks and recreation for urbanites to fawn over. Or, slithering all hilljack in camo and Copenhagen, streaked with face paint, past the swingset. Diving behind the beauty bush, then nocking an arrow, and drawing back statuelike by the sign that says all dogs must be on a leash. Is it apropos to test the wind through the gate of the upscale community, before driving an arrow through the maw of a bad boy city buck that's tiptoeing toward the halo of the streetlight?

I don't question my pal even now because I enjoy his company and respect his otherwise learned hunting prowess. I just chalk up the deer head as giving in to a moment of weakness, even though it was planned.

For months.

He owns a fine deer head. And I'm positive it has more gray on its chin and around its ears than when I first saw it unboxed.

It certainly adds a modicum of charm to an old farmhouse.

Besides, had the deer not been so massive and faulty in its judgment, taking the easy path through its short and happy life, mind you, by living on the edge of a popular neighborhood, garden feeding and fattening itself on marigolds and cucumbers, my pal wouldn't have popped it.

Destiny definitely played a part.

If he ever plans to sell that mount, I'll take it. If only for the story it is not allowed to tell.

Small Rigs Are Good Bets In Idaho's Big Places

I have a friend who drives an early '90s-model Toyota pickup with mud on the doors and downy feathers embedded in the back seat.

The pickup truck was purchased second hand, but new enough when it seemed plausible that the two-door regular cab was a necessary payout for a job that required tooling backcountry roads from the Snake River to the fringes of Lolo Pass, north to the Larkins, or the nose of Montana.

The rig has, over the years, carried in its confines deer and elk, chukar, pheasant, grouse, salmon and two dogs that are going gray.

It's been a pretty good pickup truck, my friend mulls. A few of its parts have gone missing over time, have been broken or clanked loose and lost on gravel roads that are slick with mud or snow or the chowder-hungry grind of road dust that in summer, mountain dew can't touch.

Some of the best hunting and fishing vehicles are the

ones so innocuous they appear to be push-overs, easy to thumb a nose at, making them stealthy in their approach to things outdoors.

His no-frills beater is among them.

And so is the Subaru Forester with 270,000 miles on the odometer that a guy in Montana drives into the woods each autumn because it is reliable, dingproof, and can hold an elk on the roof in a pinch.

He was fortunate once to kill a bull on the sidehill of a logging road and got the massive animal tied down, up top, with the help of ingenuity.

Because a highway through a college town was the fastest route home, he was seen midweek at rush hour, scowling behind the wheel as passersby gave him the thumbs-up for his success, or heckled him through rolled up windows. Their chagrin at his perceived gall for toting a dead wild animal on the top of his car was too much to hold back and not something his wild beard or Grateful Dead sticker could ameliorate.

A fishing guide in Dillon used to meet his clients standing outside his outdated minivan with a blue, rubber raft tied to its roof as he brushed away his white whiskers to better sip Bud Lite from a can.

At all hours.

No one begrudged him the minivan. The beard. The raft on the roof. Or his Bud Lite.

He found fish.

That's what mattered.

And he was colorful.

A pal in Livingston has a soccer mom automobile as well. It is silver, two-door, with a slider and has a hitch to trailer the raft he uses to fish the Yellowstone. A minivan by nature is spacious, providing room to keep the coolers. Everyone who rides along remains well hydrated on the river, and can stretch their legs on the ride back to town.

Mode of transportation matters less than the outing, although advertisements would have you believe otherwise, and that's good too.

But I prefer semi-compact and vintage Asian all-wheel drives with high miles and a lot of rattles when I roll into the hills after deer or elk, or any other endeavor that allows me to simultaneously pack a firearm and binoculars into a lot of quiet.

Those cars usually make room for the dog. They provide traction and are easy to park to allow logging trucks to pass on the two tracks.

They can be pushed or towed in the event they break down, but many of them seem to run forever.

And that's a good insurance policy out there where satellites mix with the stars at night, but don't give up cell service.

SOMETIME, IDAHO

Chukars On The Heels Of Heroes

There are many reasons to miss a flying chukar with a burst from a swinging shotgun, and I find hunters are too hard on themselves.

"Just a bunch of bad luck," one gruffed recently, after spending a day unable to knock down the few birds that squirted downhill into the Snake River Canyon on whirly wings in front of his dog.

"If I were better shot we could have some chukars," the other pined as he considered one particular shorthaired pointer, still not weary despite charging up and down hills that resembled the steeply-carved ridges of corduroy pants.

The pointer had climbed up and down, and up and over, and then back down again after birds that blasted from lava-rock crags toward the river before scrambling back up the steep slopes on thin, red legs like a herd of myna birds.

We didn't hear their calls.

Not very often, anyhow, and if we did, it was too late.

Chukar are known for their social calling, back and forth to nearby kin neighboring in the hills.

What they tell each other with the lamentful chuk-ah, chuk-ah is anyone's guess, but it's likely they aren't talking about the weather.

Which was windy that day on the Snake River breaks not far from Lewiston, and across the river from Asotin, Wash.

Asotin, by the way, is a tiny town known for its old courthouse and because it is home to Jesse Davis. He was a University of Idaho gridiron hero who landed a spot on the Dolphins O-line after playing for a spell for the Seahawks.

It is also where Coeur d'Alene hero and former police sergeant Greg Moore, a biology major who loved to hunt and fish, got his start as a deputy.

Moore was later gunned down by a drug addict in Coeur d'Alene while he patrolled a residential neighborhood.

A water structure in the city's park bears his name.

Asotin is the self-proclaimed steelhead and chukar capital of Asotin County and it's as far as you can get from Seattle without leaving the state.

Here's a secret: People formerly of Seattle live there for this reason.

Big, wild sheep roam nearby, along with large-antlered mule deer. Rattlers skitter in the rocks, and the creek that runs through town was a place where Nez Perce people once harvested, for the delicate meat, the lampreys that S-curved up the free-flowing river and into the small stream to spawn.

Mark Allen, a tribal member who had his hair cut once

each week at the local barbershop in Lewiston until his death at 84, remembered the lampreys from his childhood and kept them with the hunting, fishing and berry picking tales of his boyhood.

He had hunted chukar too, and smiled when he thought about it.

The day we hunted was windy and relatively cold in the banana belt of the Snake country. No one thought about berries, or lampreys, or rattlers for that matter as our small hunting party picked its way across loose rock and the tussles of thin grass where chukars like to keep a sentry before calling, running away or whirring up and then wheeling downhill, as they catch wind, like small TERCON missiles, hugging contour.

I took a couple shots as well from my over and under cannon. The first shot was just to loosen up the bottom barrel of the 12 gauge, and to test my footing, which wasn't very good, but the second shot had a chance.

The gun went boom, twice, in quick succession because chukars, Asian imports that came to town a half century ago from the rocky canyons of places like Turkey, expect it.

They expect you to shoot at them. That is why, when you miss, they run back uphill to be shot at again.

I am unsure if their small, finch-like beaks can crack a smile, but I believe they are giddy at the prospect of being gunned, and they may have a death wish, which keeps things exciting given the bland surroundings.

"You would too, if you lived in these God-forsaken hills,"

said a friend who owned a lapdog, but didn't bring it along.

Oh well, I thought.

"What do you mean?" The guy with the pointer said. "Lookit this view!"

He then waved his free arm to keep his balance and catch his footing.

The blast from my second shot — the one I thought had a chance but didn't drop a bird, pushed me back against the hillside and I felt like I was lying down, but I was more or less standing up because of the steepness.

I got grass on the back of my jacket.

Hunting for Idaho chukars doesn't end until sometime in winter.

I may head down to Riggins. It's steep country there, too, with lots of birds, I'm told. That small town is a whitewater rafting capital and known for a guy named Leighton Vander Esch. Just a kid who likes to hunt and fish and chase quarterbacks while playing for America's team.

You know who I mean.

He's probably missed a few birds too. It's part of the game.

Bird Dogs Willing To Put Up With Their Owners

I heard a story about a bird dog that couldn't be trained and usually ran off flushing pheasants and Huns a quarter-mile away in the wrong direction. One day the dog, an English pointer, sprinted off after scent and its owner sighed, realizing he would get rid of the darned dog as soon as he returned to the ranch. Maybe trade him for a weaner pig, a lame ewe or a one-legged hen.

Then, just when the dog was barely visible on the horizon it flushed a brace of pheasant. The roosters flew up, cackled and caught a breeze. They flew toward the man, who was unprepared for this bouquet of good fortune.

He kneeled by a fencerow of wait-a-minute vine and the birds kept coming.

He jacked a shell into the chamber of his scattergun.

The birds kept coming.

He flipped the gun's safety switch with a thumb.

They quit pumping their wings and set them instead, into a glide.

They were heading directly toward the field edge and the hedge the man used as cover when, from a kneeling position, the man shot both of the birds as they passed overhead like ducks locked on a set of decoys.

It was a good day.

He kept the dog.

Paging through gun dog magazines I am often attentive to the names of the canines and their ostensible cunning, pleasant demeanor and lack of flash. These are just plain solid dogs, obviously well mannered, with instincts as sharp as razor wire and photogenic even when caught leaping into water bristling with fraggle ice. They are dogs my pals and I could hope to find maybe once in our lives for a season, if luck held out, until their real owners came to claim them.

We once found a chocolate Lab, in a field with a farmhouse a half-mile away, and hunted rabbits with it before taking it home.

It had a nose for loping cottontail that hid in the hawthorn and red osier dogwood, and the hare that busted loose from the still standing patches of swamp grass.

Poor lost baby. Not a bad pup. Fair nose. Par on the retrieve. We fed it cans of veal and liver and probably would have named it Lancelot, or Bruiser if the farmer hadn't called and asked for his dog back.

"Neighbor said you might have got my lab."

"Um, what neighbor?"

"A guy named Scurvy, out on the Mud Loop Road, said he

recognized one of you boys from the football team."

"Huh."

"So, you got my dog?"

"Maybe ... what's she look like?"

We awkwardly tottered in his driveway later, hands in our pockets, moving in and out of the gray shade that seeks to decipher perverse or good intentions until the farmer generously adjudicated, "Feel free to come hunt with her anytime. She needs the exercise."

A friend of mine named his English pointer for the first game it flushed. We hunted an overgrown logging road when the pup nosed into a stand of alder and kicked out a cow and calf moose that trotted our way on high legs, apparently miffed. "Moose!" My friend yelled, and the pup came running as we scattered into the nearby trees for whatever cover we could find.

Because there were many moose that year sharing ruffed grouse cover, this scenario repeated itself and turned into sort of a habit. He yelled, "Moose!" And the pointer, ears pinned back and tail tucked, beat a path to its owner's side, as the owner beat a path for cover.

Moose, the pointer, grew up big, and he liked to hog the front seat of the Jeep Wrangler that my friend drove to hunting spots in eastern Washington, Idaho and Montana.

Like a lot of dogs of this breed, Moose became a nonconformist as a teenager, preferring to range far from adults — and he may have punched his ticket in all three states by himself in an afternoon, but we could never be sure.

The practice continued into his later life. He usually returned to us worn out, dragging his tongue, but in good spirits. A few quail feathers stuck to the side of his mouth, and he slept the entire drive home.

This was before my buddy had children. Children consider a working dog a digit of their extended family, which prevents its sale no matter how inept the mutt is in the field. When my friend traded his dog for an over-under shotgun, I noticed the blood pressure pills disappeared from his medicine cabinet, and he took a certain pleasure hunting over other people's dogs. When their pooches displayed bad form, ate birds, failed to fetch or forgot their raison d'etre, he did not offer advice or critique. Without a dog, he had become a gentleman, almost a squire, who held his gun gracefully at port arms ready for a flush, instead of swinging it about like a bull rider as he had when he scanned the horizon for his errant bird hound. He now chatted amicably and astutely. Even his vocabulary changed.

But that was years ago.

When I spoke to him the other day, I noticed a sharper edge to his usually tempered demeanor and just a modicum of grit sprinkled his former flowery attitude. His mien hearkened back to the old days when Moose disappeared into the next county until suppertime.

I heard a whimper in the background.

"What's up?" I asked.

"Not a whole lot," he pined. "Got a new dog."

"Really? That's nice. How's it hunting?"

There was a pause like the one when we stood in the farmer's driveway with our hands in our pockets years ago searching the horizon for words to express something non conveyable.

"The kids really like it," he ventured.

It's a Lab, he said. It's amazing how fast they become part of the family.

SOMETIME, IDAHO

Winter

SOMETIME, IDAHO

More Than Tine

This whole antler hunting thing started with a whitetailed deer shed found in a stand of cedar behind the house one spring when I was eight.

I kept the antler on a chest of drawers wondering how exactly I could get another one.

In the flat, lake country where I lived, whitetailed deer moved from island to island, lake to lake and kept mostly to the cedar hollers and tamarack bogs in winter, but I didn't think to look there.

I found a couple more shed antlers randomly while hiking through deep overgrowth and others I found years apart along fencerows poking from winter grass that hid them like maiden hair.

A pair of fresh, brown whitetail sheds lay 10 feet apart under a pine, but it's usually not that easy.

When I moved the mountains I discovered that an antler can sometimes be seen for a hundred yards from a ridge top.

I knew a man who spent days hunting the shore of a lake in early winter. He filled boxes with antlers that were dropped by whitetailed deer where the snow was sparse said that place is over-hunted now, and I haven't talked to him in years.

Backwoods dirt bike riders deride shed tine. They toss dropped antlers into thickets so knobby tires won't be punctured.

Sometimes you misstep and have a shed antler lacerate your leg before you notice it.

My neighbor who worked as a sawyer felling trees for a logging company, lifted a pant leg and showed me a scar. The heavy five-point antler that made the mark with a saber like G-3 lay now on the roof of a lambing barn with other antlers he found over the years. He had stepped on it while notching a tree, and its dagger point scarred his flesh under a pant leg above the laces of a caulked boot.

Turkey season is a good time to find sheds.

On my first turkey hunt when spring gobbler tags were a desired commodity, I slyly slipped into a small clearing where the sun cut a hole in the snow. A six-point elk shed — just one side — lay new and nut brown in the warm spring grass as if religiously placed. It was the color of walnut. I quit hunting gobblers and carried the trophy a mile back to the car.

One particular moose antler picked from the snow was given to a pal who accompanied my shed hunt that day. We spent hours trudging in seeming aimless circles through a sleet shower, post-holing through the icy crust of an aspen grove at the edge of a mountain. We climbed, switch-whipped, through brush fields stopping only to sip water and chew apples down to the seedy core for sustenance. He keeps the palmate shed with a beam like a rifle stock on a mantle in his house, because it is that kind of trophy.

All of them are.

Horns, as we call them, are more than bone.

They are the things they carried, so to speak, the weapons of the gracious, hooved beings we hunt in autumn, sometimes just to sneak up close to watch them without shooting. There are times we pursue animals for weeks, just for a glimpse.

You can't eat horns our friends' fathers used to say. They meant a hunter should be after meat, not regalia, or trappings, or odds and ends. But hunters who chase tine know it rewards you twice.

Every antler tells the story of an animal that can be chased again, and there is mystery, too, in tine.

When Carl Sandburg asked the bluebird, "What do you feed on?" He was saying that, as a poet, he visually fed on the bird's sky blue feathers, the magical trill of its song, its dance over yellow fields, the crunch of the grasshoppers in its beak, the distance it crossed and the wind that carried it.

We feed on antlers like that.

A trio of brothers from Pinehurst hunt sheds in winter with the same diligence they use to chase elk and deer in the fall.

They go together to secret spots. They go at night and wait until light. It's a blood pact and they don't show their hand because the world is filling up with people, and they want, at least for a while, to live in a North Idaho they knew as kids.

So they use stealth and speak to no one about their antler hunting locales, and if you see them out there, they will chew gum, talk politely about the weather, sip a soda, have engine trouble, but need no help. When you're down the road out of sight, they will haul the many pounds of brown elk and deer sheds to the bed of their pickup trucks and drive home to feel them with rough hands in their garage with the door rolled down, silently lauding the animals that carried them.

By mid-to-late January whitetails for the most part have dropped their headgear. Elk, not yet, but soon.

I once met a 5x5 bull on a gravel road in May as I rounded a turn. It surprised us both. He lept over a fence and through low-limbed trees that didn't knock loose his rack.

A friend says Easter is the best time to hunt sheds.

It doesn't matter when you go.

You can learn a lot about the woods just by walking it, and there's always plenty of tine for that.

The Religion Of Solid Ground

If you find yourself in a car careening across the ice of a frozen lake this winter, you may do well to keep the door ajar, if only for the sake of the guy riding shotgun who yells, "Crack your door!"

It won't save you when the 1982 Monte Carlo goes through the ice, though.

Neither will rolling down your windows, I am told.

It's cold outside and if you break through on your way to your favorite ice-fishing hole, you may as well drown in comfort while the heater is turned on high.

When the guy in the middle of the bench seat, with his knees jammed against the dashboard and his stocking cap pulled down to his chin, starts whispering chants to a greater deity that sound like a repetitive hankering for Cheez-its, take heart. He's not hungry. Just 20 minutes ago he ate three jalapeno corn dogs from the glass case at the Quick Mart where you stopped for bobbers, lead sinkers, maggots and gasoline. And now, of all things forsaken by the ghost of Roy Orbison you've suddenly found yourself way out on the lake with the nose of the '82 Monte pointed directly at a dot that seems like a distant planet in a cold, unfeeling universe.

The dot is an ice house. Others call it a fish house. Inside, anglers sit on cushions as they try to catch fish through holes quietly and without fuss.

It is a safe place, despite its great distance across a white surface of barren lake ice that someone proclaimed — was it the guy at the bar? — is thick enough for a bulldozer.

The dot is your destination.

The last land beacon, a lone pine on a fading shoreline, is getting smaller, falling almost out of eyesight.

But thank God for the all-season radials, right? They speed you over the wind-blown surface of snow that separates the dot from the chassis you occupy with two men in pack boots and mittens who pressed you into service.

"Let's go fishing!" They exalted earlier in the day, but their enthusiasm has waned with the sound of splitting ice.

Whether the groans are from a lot of ice, or a thin layer of ice is being loudly contested by the psychedelic noises that emanate from underneath the car. They sound like the entire polar ice cap is ripping apart, and the car stereo turned up loud can't mask them. The sweet hum of the 305 V8 under the metallic green hood of the Monte can't appease the wailing of ice that will inevitably break open like a maw and eat all of you, leaving nothing but steam and a gaping hole full of cubes.

And then you feel them.

They are what ice fishermen collectively call the jitters.

The jitters happen when you've been on the ice too long during a warm spell and you look around and realize all the other anglers are gone. The last pickup is leaving the parking lot on shore a quarter-mile away and around you the crappies and bluegills you caught that morning float in three inches of water as the noon sun beats a straight path to glacial meltdown.

Your knees vibrate like a xylophone.

Jitters.

They come when the ice you're walking on rises and falls like a water bed and your boots break through the top layer of junk and hit the layer underneath without solace. The shoreline has become a temple of prayer where you will forever, if you reach it, live a life of gratitude and charity.

You will no longer curse, you promise, but will tithe regularly. You'll join the church choir and maybe even forsake sour cream and onion potato chips.

Forever! Pleath, pleath, pleath!

Now, all of those deals you cut and failed to consummate have come to roost, haven't they? With promises scattered like empty Lay's sour cream and onion wrappers at your feet you realize life has become one big, fat gotcha!

You press the gas and beeline toward Buggy's fish house as the ice underneath the Monte howls and yowls and screams, and you unlatch and open your car door just a little. You crack it.

It won't help.

You are absolutely certain of this.

Nonetheless, you unlatch the door and the ice noise is louder, and the wheels go crunch, crunch and when you pull up beside Buggy's ice house and step from the car the jitters fade. The whimpering of the men with whom you shared the bench seat has been silenced by catharsis.

You step outside as knees tremble, just a little, and look at them.

"Chicken shit," you mouth, but you have momentarily lost your voice.

Gathering the maggots, sinkers and bobbers from the dashboard you knock on the ice house door with a shaky fist.

It is winter somewhere in the middle of the frozen, North American continent.

The sun is bright.

You stomp your feet on the ice. It's solid. The meter of your confidence rises.

Knock, knock, knock.

"Honey, we're home," you manage to sing.

Leaded Or Less So, Joe

They are ceramic, or hard vinyl, with a picture of a pheasant, a bugling elk or a bass dancing on its tail over lily pads.

If the cups are ancient, the images appear foggy as old headlights.

They aren't openly considered, these coffee cups we purchased at yard sales or gas stations. We sip from them without paying them much mind, except in the morning when the coffee pot beeps and the liquid is poured into them under a halo of steam.

Their heat feeds us then subconsciously. It reminds us what it's like to be outside under a dripping cedar bough waiting for deer to sneak from a canyon, or to watch our wake as we idle from the harbor. We should be wade fishing, casting in front of a rock where the current runs through the shade, or climbing, or hiking or birdwatching, instead of doing today whatever it is that has us corralled.

It is with the whispering voice of an old pal that the cups nudge a common denominator.

My coffee cups are covered in trout flies. But only one per cup, because I keep it classy.

Inside these coffee-carrying orbs with the handles usually big enough to make room for a few fingers, a stain dark as a chestnut paints the ceramic.

It glosses the inside of a favorite cup that dons a caddis fly and was part of a four-piece set.

The Royal Wulff mug too is used on occasion, but the Adams, once a top choice, has been glued like a mosaic after a wreck.

My daughter, a while back, walked off with the chartreuse humpy that probably imitated a green drake and when I see her my mantra is always the same.

"Take care of that cup," I tell her.

There are forces about, often in the form of relatives, spouses maybe, who want to snatch these cups from under the car seat, or the shop bench or from their hiding place behind the computer module on the office desk, and soak them in the dishwasher, to make them appear new again.

But that defeats the purpose doesn't it?

The coffee tannins, days, weeks or months worth, imbue our cups with a certain essence and the distinction of being seasoned. They mark time.

Each stratified layer is from a morning when we watched the steam rise while considering ambient temperature, wind chill, currents, hatches, rubs and scrapes, gobbles, yelps, wallows or swales, and tree stands, before the impending commute to work.

Each thin veneer is a promise.

These are not stains, by any stretch, but dreams, however brief, the sediments left by thoughts of being out there, and the affirmation that we will once again.

Probably soon.

We hope.

Someone gave me a Ray Troll cup that showed gargantuan Pacific salmon grinning near the rim, with the caption, "There's no nookie like a chinookie."

It broke after falling from the dashboard on a bumpy road and tangling with a hydraulic jack I kept on the floorboards for reasons I don't remember.

The cup was cheery, combining wit and the comic enthusiasm with which we sometimes view our outside exploits. It was almost too smart for the morning Joe.

The fall from the dashboard killed the Troll cup. When I got another later, of smallmouth under a Bass Ackwards design, I vowed to care for it, but it cracked too, under similar circumstances. I bound the breaks with super glue and deemed the cup unuseable for beverages, filling it instead with pens, which later turned its insides blue.

A better fit, I think.

We don't talk openly about these cups, but we consider them in that place between memory and future. Each morning when our brains work at 12 wave cycles per second these cups speak to us, their tannin layers remind us of time passing, and times past and what's out there at this moment, or later today. Their pictures tell us stories of where we've been and where we're going.

And the stuff inside of them, the mud, the dirt, the go juice, the wakey up and cuppa brew, it's just the fuel to get us there.

From Honer's Dad To You: A Good
Wish For A New Year

Most of my pal Honer's meals started with onions frying in a pan.

If it was the bass we caught, or the panfish, there was flour and a hot skillet and then the onions from a bin, sliced thick with a kitchen knife that was the biggest thing in the skinniest drawer under the counter with the linoleum print. The onion pieces were dropped into a skillet the size of a hubcap — large enough to scramble a meal for the family's four growing boys, along with mom and dad. Frying grease was kept in a bowl by the stove.

Honer's mom was usually at work at the state health and welfare office while his dad, a Korean war veteran, spent a lot of time in the garage when he wasn't employed at the local boat building yard or sitting at the corner tavern if the money held. Maybe, and quite possibly, he was off in the hills dragging deer from farm fields marked with no-hunting signs meant for people from the city who came out each year to mistake horses and cows for big game animals.

The signs were not meant for neighbors looking to put food on the table. Honer's dad insisted on this distinction.

The rules he recognized were mostly unwritten. His difficulty was with the ones printed in the game department handbook published with the punctuality of a court clerk.

One of the rules that kept the binoculars on the dashboard of the game warden's unmarked vehicle pertained to hunting spring ducks: It was not legal and could, if a judge insisted, require a spring hunter to cough up some legal tender.

To Honer's dad, legal tender was a piece of finely cooked wild game meat regardless of where or when it was got. It sizzled and turned golden at the edges when the temperature was right. It may have been perilously rare for others, but Honer's dad had a family to feed. His prowess extended to the skillet and many of his cuts spent little time with the flame before they were salted and devoured piping hot.

Hunger pangs are quelled this way.

Honer, the oldest boy and my best pal sat behind the steering wheel in the car for a quick getaway as the old man slipped through a barbed wire fence in March and sloshed across a flooded field to the cattail edge of a pond he knew before his Army days. The crack of the 12 gauge spitting lead meant that greenheads, returned from the winter bayous to feed in that snow-melted, northern grain country, would flop in the back seat of the Impala almost table ready.

"Slide over," Honer's dad would say, as he slipped his wet

countenance onto the bench seat behind the wheel of the Impala, plugged a smoke into his perpetual grin with still-wet fingers, and pushed the lighter in.

With a wet boot pressed against the gas pedal, the tawny-colored, four-door spit gravel to the next slough or flooded ag field out there in that logger-slash farm country where the old man was raised in a time when pictures, we believed, were black and white.

The world, however, was becoming more colorful and less amenable to subsistence hunting. Consumers and marketing moguls hand-in-hand made a high dollar sport of cashing in on the cast and blast addicts of forest and field.

My pals and I remember Honer's old man mostly with an unfiltered Pall Mall dangling from a lip as he loosed the hide of a whitetailed buck that hung from the rafters in the garage where a humming refrigerator held the Hamms, or later, after he quit, the soda pop.

He imbued us, the neighbor kids — it was a small town so we were all neighbors — with lore that ranged from the best price for shot shells, to keeping maggots warm under a lip while lake fishing in winter.

Each year around this time, Honer's dad resolved to do better and eventually he did.

He got a full-time job, spent less time in his garage tutoring neighbor kids in his own school of fish and game management, and bought beef on sale in bulky packages from the grocery store.

It's his early days my pals and I remember most, and the

quiet New Year's resolutions Honer's old man huffed into a cold fist while ice fishing, or cleaning crappies and pike or whitetailed deer in the cold of his garage, as he sipped from a can.

Do better, he said.

Commit to doing better.

And eventually we did.

Hauling Inestimable Cargo In Winter

Cliff Mooney carried his knowledge of school buses and their ability to get-go through backcountry snow, quietly on his sleeve like a coffee stain.

The former transportation supervisor for a small Idaho school district, Mooney preened his fleet of buses like a herd of 4-H Jersey cows, ensuring they were well fed, got the proper nutrition for powerful coats and teeth, and that they were groomed, orange and happy.

There was, of course a pragmatic side to his endeavors. Mooney was responsible, for almost two decades, for getting hundreds of school children from the gravel, mountain-road fringes of a rural district safely to the classroom at four schools each day, and return them home in similar fashion, warm, a day smarter and without snow in their shoes.

At this, Mooney was as near a magician as a person of civil servitude could be. He not only loved his work and excelled at it, he dotted and crossed its letters, let it live in his home, drank it with sugar and cream, and got some on his sleeve as he cross-trained in meteorology and weather science.

If you wanted to know what the weather was doing in a mountain drainage 37 miles away where his buses traveled for the children whose family he knew by name, Mooney could tell you.

For the weather, call Cliff. Superintendents did.

Sure, there were snow days. School was a few hours late sometimes to ensure county plows, which often worked nonstop it seemed for weeks at a time, had cleared what they could. Then the buses, rocking like a fishing fleet in a bumpy sea, picked up the cargo of kids who had crossed their fingers all night for a snow day.

Everyone has snow stories and anyone who relied on a school bus in the northern climes in winter can probably still smell the bench seats, the wet film on the floor and recall the fogged windows and name the bus driver at the helm.

Ray Rippentropp said he drove bus for egg money, and we knew it meant money to supplement what he made with his dairy herd. Its aroma lingered on Ray and often gave the bus a faint barnyard smell.

It also meant Ray, who had been up since 4 a.m. and would likely pore over his farm budget in his home office by lamplight that night, likely meant business.

No standing, stay seated, don't go out the back door, watch your head, and keep your voices down, were a few of the signs stenciled over the windows and doors that were meant to remind.

Ray didn't need to remind. Not much, anyhow.

He would stop a bus, turn on the flashers and with his neck bent because he was too tall for the inside, walk back wearing barn boots and a Carhartt jacket from which his wrists protruded, carrying heavy hands, to stymie shenanigans.

When Ray stopped and came walking, you hoped he wasn't looking for you.

We were pleased most of us, when the doors swung open in the half-light of morning, as snow flurried or whipped across the road, and Ray looked down at us from his jaybird seat to say, how you doin' today?

He was a picture of confidence when temperatures were lower than the visibility with roads ice covered and glowering with menace. We knew his were good hands.

A woman I know remembers her coach as the best bus driver she had, carrying a lot of players to a lot of games all over Idaho in the thick of winter. He would make short work of trips to gyms in other towns, so the girls could pile out and warm up, practice, and usually win.

"That's how we put trophies in the trophy case," he would say.

And the trip home was fast too, and safe.

He is still among the drivers at Cliff's transportation department, which won kudos for efficiency, and probably still does even though Cliff is no longer there.

It takes training to haul inestimable cargo around Idaho's back roads during all of the seasons.

And good hands.

SOMETIME, IDAHO

Freeze-Up Up North

Freeze-up means different things to different people and in the north, near the Laurentian Divide, the phrase is wrapped up in snow machines.

It has nothing to do with mosquitos, those black-hearted marauders of the inland swamps and marshes. They've been killed off long ago their notochords snapped by the first hard frost like a silken spider's web, their offspring wrapped in ice like minute mastodons.

Their long-ago buzzing is a hollow and frail memory like the nickel ice cream cones in July.

The declaration that follows freeze-up is simple: It's snow cat time again on the lake and an angler can expect water hard enough to bear the weight of a snow machine, or a tractor pulling an ice house onto any of the small-acre potholes fringed by white pine, aspen and birch that hold bluegill, crappie and bass.

Down south those water holes might be called tanks. Up

here, we refer to them as lakes because we like how that sounds especially if it has a relative's name in front of it.

Salo Lake, Madam Fry Lake, Whitey Lake or What'shernameagain Lake. Lagnaf was thought to be named for a Russian settler but it was determined later to be an acronym for something unseemly that neighbors still bashfully whispered about.

The bastardizations of family names are a tribute to souls who may or may no longer be kickin' it in the same Grain Belt beer tavern we have tenanted since our last season on the high school football team. The gridiron then was at the edge of Root Lake where all the high school games were played under the lights after the first October frost. New money moved it closer to town.

The tavern with the swinging Grain Belt sign, which creaks in an autumn gale that blows the leaves around is where we ponder ice fishing and the efficacy of fish houses built in the garages of people we have known since grammar school.

The fish houses were refurbished, some stick built, or converted from small RV camping trailers as a means to fish in comfort when the temperature dips into the zone known to freeze skin in a couple of minutes. Thirty seconds if there's a breeze.

The main endeavor then, after Thanksgiving or somewhere around Christmas is getting the fish houses on the hard water, a task more easily accomplished if snow is scant.

The challenge, daunting as it may seem to those less hearty and cold-fingered, is consummated using the tow bar

Uncle Heino made from the New Holland haybine broken and left since the 60s in the field by the tamarack swamp. It fits the ball hitch with just a little jimmy and some bouncing while you stand on it. An 8-pound sledge hammer tapped upwards from a low angle while lying in the snow on your back will pop loose the bind just fine, or use a screw jack. Each year Heino says he'll tender adjustments to ease the bite of the bar on the ball, but he hasn't yet and it doesn't really matter because the sledge is left inside the ice house in the box under a cushioned seat, which is hinged. In addition to the chunk of nine-pound, factory-made iron stamped with a seal from an Ohio foundry — hard to find in a world where industry has gone overseas — the compartment holds spare ice fishing rods and a spool of monofilament.

Also, and keep this close to your vest, incarcerated inside the compartment is a trove of secret spoons and jigs that like juju or dried chum can tease a bite from an otherwise hopeless afternoon on the ice. And there's a bottle of booze.

Heino was in Korea and is getting older and we're just glad to share a fish house with him as the blue flame of the propane heater dances and makes shadows like puppet theater on the walls insulated with pink styrofoam usually reserved for concrete work. Inside the fish-house walls, scored with a skillsaw to fit between the four-by studs, the foam, according to Heino, adds buoyancy, and provides a measure of assurance.

"Flotation," Heino says. In case the house goes in.

Meaning into the drink.

The water under the ice is 40-degrees.

A breakthrough is as unlikely, frankly, as the sighting of a great white shark muddling in a freshwater lake 600 miles north of the nearest crown stone, but we still think about it.

When you're standing on 12, maybe 18 inches of ice, and you giddily consider it could be two feet thick by morning because the mercury is falling into the little glass bulb that says five below, and you have a half pint of single-malt somewhere in the down puffed pocket of your coat, perceived danger adds fire to your stoic jubilation.

How swimmingly Landwehr, you jitter to yourself in the voice of an astronaut while sharing a bench with Heino who wears Maine Guide pants to your Johnson wools. His pack boots have been mended with bicycle inner tube patching.

In a fish house, time is measured by the ice on a bobber in the holes in the floor of the hut warmed by a propane stove.

It is the only place there is more than you want of time.

Footwear is among the topics discussed in a fish house.

Your surplus bunny boots are made of white felt and lined with thick carpet-like insulators. The boots appear comical as if you have large potatoes on your feet.

Heino says, "I bet those boots are warm."

Indeed they are, and a fine observation, dear sir.

"Probably durable too".

"Again, let me commend you."

"Sure are a good looking boot," Heino says, but he looks away and you sense a snigger that he turns into a, "Gotta bite!" as he hand lines a crappie through the hole.

Where I worked a long time ago along the coast, "freeze-up" meant that repairs were especially cumbersome wearing mittens and thick insulated coveralls, hats and air force surplus winter wear that kept your feet warm to 80 below.

When it gets that cold the machinery won't start, or at least it isn't worth messing with.

Just leave it there until break-up, headquarters might crackle over the radio. Often we obliged, stashing gear, sometimes as the snow fell like breast feathers of a gander, fast and heavy but soft, still, and quietly muffling the sound of the big diesels. It dampened voices too and hushed natural things like salt water slipping over rocks, or pushing against it. Ice formed with the quiet celebration of clinking champagne glasses. It meant soon a plate of glass would cover the bay where fresh water mingled with sea, and coerce the crew boat if we were not careful, to a complete standstill.

During these times, unfulfilled contracts prevented common sense, and that meant pits had to be shot, rock demanded hauling and the steel seats of D-8 cats were wrapped with heat tape. At least until breakdowns became intolerable and the boss secured an extension on the work until spring. Then the cat skinner coiled up his heat tape, stuffed it into a coffee can and returned it to the plumbing in the uninsulated garage back home where it originated.

A supervisor I once knew decided enough was enough when he lit his backside trying to warm it by the heat of a burn barrel after spending part of a morning rebuilding a truck transmission outdoors, in a gravel pit, on an island in the falling snow.

We rolled him around to extinguish the flames but the fire ate up the part of his coveralls that were needed to keep hypothermia away, he said, so we all went home until May.

The oceanic bay we traversed to get out of camp that December was a wintering ground for gray whales and they were hard to see in the blistering, freezing rain.

Because the windshield was iced over, we navigated by an early model GPS anticipating that Moby Dick may lurk on the other side of each wave.

A few whales porpoised, but not near enough to capsize the crew boat.

Good times is an aphorism used when we have forgotten how churlish things get in the cold.

A North Idaho man I know hunted mule deer only after the roads were blocked with snow and the high country was inaccessible to anyone without a snowmobile, or good webs and big lungs. He traversed to the tops of mountains with familiar names, returning to glass sometimes for days until he found a deer he wanted to kill, and then he really got moving. Winter is hard on many things, and the lack of light makes living out of doors taxing. That he was successful much of the time speaks to his will and passion for blacktails.

A logging truck driver in St. Maries who bought his rifles custom-made in Spokane spent winters trapping so far away from landlines and blacktop that he had difficulty explaining his reverence for the solitude of such places. They are isolated beyond measure, wind-blown and left to traveling predators because the snow pack, 12 feet deep is hard as a highway system.

The oldest and most massive deer, elk and moose, he said, spent winters in the high country.

He mistook the first wolf he saw up there for a domestic dog and he looked for its owner. There were more wolves the following year.

After that he said the antlered ungulates disappeared from those wind-blown elevations because wolves walked on snow while moose, blacktail and elk had to plow through it. They met their demise eye to eye.

"It was a killing ground," he said.

When his father asked him to leave a map to mark his whereabouts in case of an accident, the man said, "Dad, if anything happens to me out there between Clarkia and Montana you'll never find me anyhow."

The country is thousands of square miles and in the winter satellite pictures show it contourless, just a massive scab of hardened snow, white as a blanched filet of halibut.

Sometimes when I'm standing in my driveway in my stocking feet in the morning holding the newspaper, I wonder what it was like up there for him back then, but I do not dally because frost and my thinly-clad feet don't get along. The cement is cold and the morning gray, and grass blades in the yard are icy little spears. It's apparent that the days of comfortably hunting in running shoes are over.

When it arrives, teeth-chattering weather means different things for different people.

It means the woods are quieter, fewer people and machines venture into them and the sound of snowshoes on freshly-fallen powder is curiously akin to breathing.

The cold brings opportunity, which in this liquid we call time is taken advantage of only by the mindful. It is among the reasons we sit in the ice house with Heino.

Cold Enough For Ya?

I tiptoed down to the living room and peered outside at the thermometer.

Then I tiptoed back upstairs so as not to wake the dog.

"It's 1 degree out," I whispered to her in a library voice.

Lying on her stomach, with a pillow over her head, she took the bait.

"Aarmpf," she said.

Then I let her have it.

"That means," I said, pausing for effect, keeping my voice low and steady, "It's 7 degrees below zero with the windchill."

It was probably shock that kept her from immediately bolting upright.

"Arpf," she replied, barely audible, in her sleep.

I let the severity of this revelation sink in and tiptoed back to the kitchen so as not to wake the dog.

It was 5 a.m.

I clucked gleefully, as I planned my next move.

Long underwear? Probably.

Scarf? Maybe.

Facemask? Good idea, and good luck finding it.

Socks, gloves, coffee? All, check.

Ice cleats. Not available.

I was ready to hit the pavement, which was covered, as it were, with a slick, hard pack like a bobsled course, but damn the torpedoes, right?

When I closed the front door behind me, not much outside had changed from the night before. The air was quiet. A few cars trundled past on the main road. The snow in the yard looked as if it were part of a manger scene. The strings of heat from neighboring chimneys climbed like snakes from a basket into a sky where stars twinkled. Then the smoke and steam flickered as if in hesitation in a breeze that nicked over the treeline.

It was cold as all get out.

For some reason, as I get closer to my senile years, I like the cold as much as I think I did as a kid, when maybe I didn't like it much at all, but spent most of my time in it anyhow because, well, it was winter in a decade of lousy sitcoms. Some have called them the missing years because they were pretty uneventful.

There was no Woodstock, or mass protests, even the mile-long gas lines had faded away, and people again liked the president.

Ice fishing was a thing! And cable TV was dialed in.

The PS4 had not been mass marketed, so a creek behind

the house, a square-mile of woods and a field were our canvas, and we painted it.

That was the logic.

Go play, parents would say, and we obliged, because there wasn't much talking back through five layers of clothing, facemasks, hats and insulated boots.

If someone pushed you down outside, it's where you stayed.

These days I'm almost giddy when I revel at the cold and snow.

A friend who has made the walk with me throughout the Frozen North attributes this elation to maturation. As we get older, according to his logic, we realize weather is temporal, just a short reality bordering on fiction that swiftly passes, leaving us in a primordial state of looking back mostly, or analytically considering what lies ahead.

Bunk, I say.

Cold is cold. Take it or leave it.

As I stood on the front steps with the door closed behind me, I was already remembering how in times past I jogged in 5-below weather as I trained for a couple days to be a biathlete.

Those guns are expensive though, and I didn't have the shoes for it, I recalled.

Then out of the mist of morning and memory there was Freddy, a kid from grade school, chopping a hole in the river ice with a hatchet trying to retrieve a mink he had caught in a trap. Its $15 pelt could be the difference between a new bike in the spring with a bar between the seat and handlebars, instead of his sister's mint green hand-me-down.

Looming over Freddy and me, the sky was glass and cloudless. The moon was a pinpoint.

"Run back to the house and get the axe," hissed Freddy, who was bigger and older than me, and who liked to punch me in the arm real hard.

I ran.

It was probably 5-below back then, also. I don't recall wind, except what whirled behind me as I sprinted a half mile or more through the woods back to his house for the axe.

I found it in his garage and sprinted back down over the hard pack snow to the river.

Freddy and my friendship didn't last. But a certain love of the cold survived.

Seven degrees below zero, according to the weather charts, is a temperature that is "very cold and very uncomfortable."

Standing on the steps much older, at an age my neighbor says goes hand-in-hand with wisdom, I felt the icy burn and set out to test my attachment to discomfort.

Christmas For The Birds

He hunted with his brothers and dad on Christmas Eve and the morning after, but that was long ago, he said.

The fields were usually lightly snow-dusted with bird tracks at the edges that let the hunters know what to expect.

He remembered that part.

This was around Ephrata, Washington, a place I regard as scrubland speckled with sage and rim rock. Others, farmers mostly, consider it a good place to raise a lot of things, including hay, wheat, grapes and apples. As long as there's irrigation, the high desert will bloom.

That's what he said over coffee, when he started to recollect. He no longer lives there.

It was his stories that like a swirl of cream in coffee mixed utility with the newly imaginable. His memories of hunting the edges of tilled fields, and birds cackling skyward in a burst of flamelike exuberance got my attention like a stick-tight in a shirt collar.

Wylie and his clan didn't run dogs on the Huns and chukar and pheasants they chased often around Christmas through orchards and along the lips of wheat fields where the tall grass tipped downhill, making small tunnels that hid coveys and the occasional rooster.

The men walked three or four abreast, and a couple of them would fan out, acting like a brace of flushing dogs, anticipating a busted bird would veer within gun range.

After a fresh snow, Wylie said, the hunters drove roads behind municipal gravel trucks that sprinkled grit to give cars traction on an otherwise slippery surface. The sand from the trucks was favored by game birds that staged in the road ditches before dashing up to peck and fill their crops with the abrasive granules that helped them digest the seeds they ate.

Knowing the birds would flock along roads after a snow made finding them a lot easier in that big land where he and his party carried choked 12 gauges to better reach the ones that flushed too early. The big gauge pushed more BBs and powder and its tremendous report made the men come alive, and they were glad to be together.

Wylie who earned felony prison time for his association with a large quantity of cannabis, can no longer carry a gun, but he likes to recall the times when he could, and chasing birds is among the things he misses.

If you go, he said. Tell me how it turns out.

I had to wait a couple days after meeting Wylie over coffee for an opening. In the meantime I scrounged under the car seat, the back of dresser drawers, inside boots parked outside the mudroom door. I searched the glove box and in garage totes and old coats to recover a handful of 12 gauge shells chambered for my 3-inch tube. I don't use the Mossberg 500 a lot anymore, but Wylie's stories made me long to pack an 8-pound gun along the mucky edges of tilled fields looking for the pheasants I knew would be there.

When the opening came days later, I let the dog into the back of the SUV and sped south toward the rolling farm country of the pea and lentil capital of North America.

Somewhere around Lenville I loosed the pointer, whose whining as he stretched his nose out a cracked window had become insufferable. A Fish and Game warden parked along the road told me that this particular piece of farm-leased public land held a lot of birds earlier in the season. He had come away disappointed however when he hunted it yesterday, flushing just one grouse from brushy cover that poked into a field on the other side of an 80-acre expanse of wheat stubble.

We had not planned to hunt there, and instead had eyed a high field as we drove the canyon road that led to this place, a whole section of land open to hunting.

The little shorthair shyly stopped his incessant whining and waited obediently for the roadside conversation to end so he could bust loose in no particular direction until his tongue flopped out like a geoduck.

Ten minutes later at the corner of the hunting area along a paved road he locked up, but the rooster flew north onto private land, so we just watched as it pumped its wings before locking into a glide. We marked its landing spot out of habit and for a few seconds guessed the direction it would run, or where it would hunker and then we turned and climbed through a slick of pines to the tilled plateau of ground that stretched to a swale and out of sight.

Knowing a bird will bust from a fencerow is like watching butter melt on waffles. You anticipate the goodness and salivate in a mental way that doesn't involve taste buds. Although, in that moment before flush and flight your nostrils whiff the dirt and dead grass, akin in some ways to the rich generosity of breakfast food.

Just before the bird breaks, a hunter inhales the day's somber perfume and then time slows, providing a window of opportunity to raise the gun, if it is called for. You eye the bird as you look over the barrel and prepare to tap a trigger.

Walking toward a dog locked on point, slipping your thumb over the safety mechanism you feel your still-calm heart beating a little faster before you tell the dog, "awright."

It's just a moment. Not measurable.

The pointer, in a low crouch, takes one step, or two, or three, staccato-like bursts of energy following its torpedo nose and just ahead of the electric wagging of its stub tail.

The rooster cackles and jumps skyward, its red face patch and blue head strain in a moment of self preservation. Its crown feather catches wind and the wings whirr in front of the long, graceful tail that is the color of duck canvas or a ribbon torn from a Filson pant leg. It gains altitude before sallying forth across an open ocean of autumn earth.

Invariably, the bird's one golden eye, the one you can see, is looking at you like the eye of a trout on the hook.

The bird then becomes a slap of paint from the brush of Jackson Pollock, if artistry is something you follow. It's orange underbelly and white neck ring are stamped as if in a picture.

If you're a good shot, or lucky, like me, you notice by feel the stock tucked into the nape of your shoulder and how it jolts once, maybe twice. You hear the percussion, but barely. You anticipate the bird, it is all you're watching, fold and tumble, or just stop: Its wings stop, and its tail stops. It's as if the bird's wings are the flap of an envelope sealing shut. The bird is a parcel beautifully packaged dropping to a doorstep as the dog leaps to retrieve it.

Wylie remembered that part too. All of those roosters are somewhere tucked in his mind's eye, he said, their graceful rust-colored tails, pushing sky.

And the meals that the birds became afterward in a warm kitchen, are part of the Christmas memories a lot of hunters make.

Most memorable for me is the dog and its joyous abandon turned business, as it points and creeps to corner a bird, before the rooster vaults skyward.

"You never had dogs?"

"Never needed them," Wylie said. " But I love watching them work."

These are Christmas memories worth owning.

SOMETIME, IDAHO

Shed Hunting For The Rest Of Us

Someone said if you're not bumping into trees, or getting scratched and poked by brush and branches, you might not be shed antler hunting.

People in my neighborhood call it horn hunting because it has always been called that.

I knew I was shed hunting when my glasses fogged. Then the stocking cap covering my ears, a University of Idaho hat missing a tassel that my son purchased with savings a few years ago at a Vandals game, was pulled by a sassy limb from my head.

I got poked in the eye by a forlorn sprig of ocean spray, and then bumped headlong into a fir pole because nearby tines jabbing through the snow foretold a whitetail shed:

It looked like a four pointer. Psych!

It turned out however to be a barkless, basket-shaped limb with sticker points lying on the ground under the snow. Not an antler at all. Good luck with that, pal.

Animals don't hang around ocean spray, I told myself, so I am probably looking in the wrong place.

It's OK to talk to yourself while horn hunting, because no one's the wiser, and the only one arguing with yourself is yours truly.

Let's face it. Other horn hunters go where antlers lie in the snow like fluffy, barking puppies. Big as rodeo barrels. Some of them have signs that blurt, Lookit over here! And some sheds, the ones other people find, are slathered with neon glow paint.

You tell yourself this as the hours pass, and are interrupted in disjointed paragraphs by wild interjections:

Here we go! Bingo! Five-pointer!

Dangit.

Another ponderosa pine limb.

Those hallelujah moments, however disappointing are interrupted by long periods of silence as you navigate blowdown, slip between standing trees, gracelessly, hump through brush or barbed wire, following old tracks maybe, or new ones or just intuition.

And often, if you're like me, you eye what is surely a branched antler, and then just as surely, it is not. This happens a lot, and you start to wonder about the shape of antlers. Why do they look so much like tree limbs? You recall the genetics you learned in the 10th grade that had something to do with moths the color of bark that did not get eaten by birds because, camo. And what about those finches with different kinds of beaks found on an island where a guy named Darwin traveled in a boat called the HMS Beagle? And before you know it, you are rummaging through your memory drawer of "Gilligan's Island" reruns, which you really can't remember from that era of sitcoms that included Archie Bunker, Mr. Kotter, Arthur Fonzarelli. Ayyy!

Your eyes scan a radius of 10 feet at a time in a field overrun by pine and buckbrush, when, Bang! You smack headlong into another tree, and a limb snags the hat from your head, and you get eye-poked because your glasses have fogged and ride in a pocket, or at the end of your nose.

I wear the Vandals hat for luck.

And I wear caulk-soled boots glued together at Hoffman's in Kellogg, Idaho, and I carry a Buck knife made exclusively down the road in Post Falls. I carry these hometown accoutrements because I know they will give me an edge, and any advantage that can tip the scale and help you become a horn hunter who gathers tine is worth its weight in bone.

I once took a friend scavenging the hills and forests for antlers and after a day he wondered dejectedly what he was doing out there, taking occasional bites from a protein bar, and bumping into trees.

I had managed to stumble upon a couple small deer sheds, but he wasn't impressed.

He longingly eyed the paddle in my hand, while blowing warmth into his own chafed and frozen paws.

So, I gave it to him. It was an impressive moose paddle from a Shiras, but I found only one side. When I handed it to him, his eyes sparkled and his frozen and chapped lips curved up at the ends.

I have a picture of him with the shed in the parking lot of a Coeur d'Alene grub pub where we went afterwards and where I thought he would barter it for beer, but my pal refrained and I'm glad he did. Antlers should not be besmirched with licentiousness, or traded for anything but reverence before they are stored away in boxes in the garage.

The paddle was the last moose antler I found, even though I have been looking. More people — 40-some percent — who put in a modicum of time trudging around the woods late winter and spring find between one and five antlers a year, according to a survey that also reported 16 percent of antler hunters find nothing, and 13 percent find fewer than 10 sheds annually. The other 29 percent find more than 10 antlers a year.

These numbers were calculated by a group of horn hunting addicts who think so hard and often about antlers that the math doesn't bother them.

Over the past decades, I have fine-tuned my antler-sensing skills, and stand firm in my belief that local, good luck juju is key to turning tine.

That's why I plan to carry a jar of Litehouse dressing made, bottled and boxed in Sandpoint, Idaho in my pack to shoehorn me into the top 29 percent.

Blue cheese. Chunky. It should complement the protein bars.

Spring

SOMETIME, IDAHO

Sometimes Idaho

He was old when I met him.

Old to me.

I was shaggy haired, a kid, and Faye's crop was white, tightly clipped, his beard grizzled, mostly gray and the skin on his arms and neck was leathery but would crinkle when he bent over to tie a boot lace. The brown spots and the lines that etched his face were the work of the sun I believed, and too much time spent under it. The skin on his arms was scaled with wiry hair and tattoos from the Navy. Anchors and women in both green and blue.

He was lean as spar.

Faye had been a timber faller. That is what we called the men who carried oily saws with long bars and skip chain, gas cans and leather tool belts that held spark plug wrenches, a screwdriver, files, wedges and a hatchet stuffed into the belt, or an axe alongside. They carried this regalia into the woods where they worked most of the day felling trees that the salty referred to as timber.

He had cut spruce and hemlock all up the coast in the days when the trucks were mostly off road. Much of the place at the time was considered "off road," even though pavement glistened in a few stretches.

State troopers regulated the pavement and kept a watch with sirens and ticket books because off-road trucks were too heavy, and could carry too many logs stacked too high.

The state capital, where the road department employees lurked in offices setting weight restrictions, calibrating gravel and shoulder width, deemed off-road logging trucks a hazard to their superior sensibilities. The truck bunks were wide enough to test fog and center lines at the same time, and the wood brazenly stacked two stories high was best left for postcard pictures.

The big diesels destroyed the road bed. Their outrageous heft sank pavement, and much of the time the trucks rode on treadless tires.

It often appeared the magnanimous loads, according to the men and women with the clip boards and wicker bill hats, were poorly secured - unlike their own government paychecks.

The drivers who navigated these machines sported attitudes deemed anti-social. The highways after all were meant for civil commerce, pedestrians, family cars, bicycles and the kind of pay-as-you-go transactions that demanded neatly-washed clothing with cuffed pants, maybe button up shirts, ties, smiles and a haircut.

The old man had felled the timber that filled the bunks

of the off road trucks and later, when he was older, he sat
in the cab behind the wheel of behemoth wood haulers
manufactured by Hayes or Pacific. Names such as Pentilla,
Olsen Log or Ketchikan Pulp were painted on the doors.

I met him on an island where we flew from the mainland
in planes with pontoons, propellers and seats with small
windows and when the tide was right we motored right
up to the float logs by the cook house of this logging camp.
Sometimes when the water was low we stayed out at the end of
the floating log booms that corralled spruce saw logs or pulp
wood neatly bundled. We waited for a kid younger than me to
meet us in a skiff pushed by an 18-horsepower Yamaha motor.
He would snatch us up, grin and say things like, "You got a
hard-on for loggin', I kin tell."

It was difficult to ascertain if the boy was a few sections
behind on the pay scale, brazen, or wiley as a peahen.

Word was he and the boss were related, so it ended there.

I met Faye again, later, in one of the towns that survived
by virtue of two industries, both of them natural because
they relied on the woods and water. Their scent bored into
nostrils. The aroma of *picea sitchensis*, the sweet pitch
that burned on the saws, mixed with oceanic brine and the
luxurious breath of salmonids: guts and eyes and fins, and the
cannery steam. Tourism existed but only as a seasonal and
fractional byproduct. Faye and I had coffee sometimes in a
cafe where people looking for work or waiting on it, sat around
small tables dipping Copenhagen. Highliner caulked shoes,
Currin-Greenes, Westco and Buffalos were among the regular

footwear, or Romeo deck shoes. Occasionally the Rainier slipper with the slim heel made in Ballard was on display. The footwear varied with the season. Many of the customers elbowing eggs and biscuits supplemented their incomes away from the woods by roiling in the cabins of double enders, or a ketch as they trolled for big-money king salmon to ensure their pay was unsigned by bureaucracy.

Faye talked mostly about his mining claims because he was either going to them or coming back when his full time work was on holiday, but it wasn't really talk. Mostly it was comprised of linguistics. Pieces of information loosely cast and mingling with the words themselves. Because the words were so few, they sought out each other's company, sometimes joining to form a sentence and at other times lingering in the form of half thoughts.

Depending on syntax and whether a concept was valued enough for conviction, the words might warrant a reply. Other times, there was less telling, so the half thoughts hung in the air like smoke from an ashtray and finding no company, simply dissipated.

"Yeah," Faye would say as a means to fill silence, or, "Well."

Words that joined each other might be something like, "I took the sluice box up to 12-Mile Creek."

And later, "Found a little color."

He had claims way up north as well, and his prospecting took him places, usually alone, that people in general and without a hunting tag wouldn't consider a destination.

Once in the spring on the glacier fed Patterson River, Faye

crossed bleak, hasty water that his experience had deemed tentative but not absolutely an impediment. Seated on a four-wheel ATV laden with camp and mining gear, Faye felt the icy current thrust against the machine and then capsize it.

It was somewhere around his birthday because he spent 67 recovering from the drenching he got in the Patterson when the four-wheeler was lifted by the current before keeling sideways. It flushed against a log jam, so Faye, in water up to his hips ran the winch that got the Yamaha back up on the bank. He drained the water from the carburetor, the chunks of ice from his boots, then limped the machine many miles back to camp where after a fitful night monitoring the radio he caught a bush plane to town and the hospital that treated him for cuts and bruises.

We sat in the cafe afterwards over coffee, biscuits and eggs, him wearing Romeos to my Xtra-Tuf rubber boots, and we watched through the window the snow that appeared to be receding from the nearby mountains. He told about the experience on the Patterson, or some of what happened, offering a summary of sorts.

"Yeah," he said. "That was something."

Faye didn't let on about his personal life. He had a wife once, and children. We, who knew Faye, were unsure how many wives or kids he loosed himself from or was tied to. He didn't say, at least not all at once, and others when asked couldn't ascertain much with any certainty either. He grew up in the Navy, he once said as a reply to an inquiry, and his home was, well, on the coast.

And Montana too.

Sometimes, Idaho, he said.

His close friends said he was a sailor. His other close friends said he was a logger, a fisherman, a miner. He had a lot of close friends, but none that knew him too much. Either that, or they shared his distaste for allocution.

His mining claims were mostly stretched from the Stikine River to northern California's yellow pine forests, and east to Idaho and Montana.

After Faye died in the pioneer home in a rural village, someone said his father was a teacher and his mother a librarian and that the family lived east near Missouri. It all made a little sense if you allowed it.

It was his imagination that fueled his passion for adventure and the only possessions Faye left behind were his tools, a pickup and the boxes of books that included Chaucer and Beowulf, dog eared copies of Lord Byron, Keats, Yeats, Shelley and others. He had some gold in a Mason jar and we found the stainless steel .44 Smith and Wesson he kept under his mattress away from the caregivers.

It was loaded, of course, because what's the sense of a gun if it ain't, Faye would have said.

The land he owned, and the claims through probate were passed to one daughter, and his youngest brother who drove an economy car from Galesburg, Illinois, to the ferry boat that made the trek to the islands. He was accompanied by a tawny cat and displayed an eye tick. He collected the boxes of books and the gold.

Marvelous the small man said, his eye ticking like a watch.

Faye's youngest brother explained some of Faye's past, repeated that he hadn't seen him in 40 years, and ruminated about the inexplicable passing of time and complication of distance. He looked around at the mountains and clouds and the towering trees with his one good eye, while his ticking eye danced an accordion tune. Then he opened his arms and said, "My God, no wonder he never came home."

The scenery was marvelous and worth sticking around for.

He drove away. Back to the land of Lincoln, someone suggested, or maybe just down the road to strike it rich on Faye's claims. We never heard again from the man.

Once with the help of some kitchen-made Schnapps that a friend let fester all winter in a bowl on top of the refrigerator, Faye laid a map of Idaho on a table and with a finger pointed to drainages the names of which have fallen away like Faye's belongings in the Patterson River.

With his finger on the forest map, he made rough circles showing a vast splash of green sparsely roaded. The immense primeval hinterlands were no obstruction to Faye, not at his age. They were an opportunity.

When will you go to Idaho? Someone asked.

Some time, Faye said. Maybe soon.

SOMETIME, IDAHO

The Golden Guide To Becoming A River Fisherman

The pocket book was not the kind you fill with money, but we hoped its pages held a different kind of jackpot, making the book worth more than the buck and a quarter we had paid for it at the drugstore.

The book, a Golden Guide, called "A Guide to Fresh and Saltwater Fishing" barely squeezed into a shirt pocket without busting a seam. It contained more than 650 illustrations, "in full color," so the best place for it was in the palm of your hand.

On its pages were drawings of curvy rivers and streams with stones placed here and there, tributaries and feeders, different kinds of debris, and amidst this blend of structure and current, it showed where to find the fish that looked like Ichthys bumper stickers in a prayer meeting parking lot.

The book made clear that by following its advice, we would certainly hook something. And we imagined kneeling on the river bank holding glistening bass or trout in our wet hands that May day when Kooch's mother drove us in the family station wagon to the river bridge a few miles out of town and promised to pick us up in a few hours.

We didn't know then that she would forget us. We were certain after the green station wagon disappeared toward town, however, that none of us carried a watch, so it didn't much matter.

We were 11 years old, the four of us, packing rods and reels, plugs, spoons and spinners, and the clouds in the sky were thin streamers when we rallied along the bridge to peer into the book.

We each memorized a scenario:

If the river made a U-turn, fish would sit in the deep current near the far bank probably holding close to the bottom waiting for food to drift by, according to an illustration in the Golden Guide.

Nuthead committed the scene to memory.

Check.

Kooch memorized the picture of a feeder stream entering the river that showed a passel of fish holding just down current.

Kopper and I kept a few diagrams too tucked in gray matter before tumbling down the embankment to the river grinning like squirrels ready to catch bucket loads of bass and sauger, a brook trout or maybe a spotted pike.

We didn't catch anything that day. Unless you count the rocks and sticks. We walked several boy miles — who knows how far. We climbed wet or dry rocks for a better presentation. We snagged or broke lines in murky side channels, on brush growing from the opposite stream bank, or under mid-current boulders. We waded after spoons or spinners hooked on rocks or submerged limbs, and rallied like a recon team in the shade of leaning pines or river birch to peer into the pages of the Golden Book expecting a secret.

The secret it didn't tell was how the state fisheries department had electroshocked that stream and planned to restock it with indigenous species. What was there now, chubs and shiners mostly and a spring run of suckers, didn't chase Daredevils, plugs or whiptail spinners.

It didn't tell us that this whole river fishing deal would become a thing. It would squirm around in our minds for many years and despite its lack of fruitfulness that spring day, it would embed itself in our brainpans like the smell of fried chicken.

We had become river anglers.

Kooch, who would play football for Montana State and sell sporting goods, and Kopper, who would become a building contractor, and Nuthead, a road construction concrete cutter, would each turn to rivers for contentment in the years to come.

That spring day, wading knee deep in sneakers, had done it.

And the Golden Book, a buck and a quarter, no batteries, but a recharge on each page and in each of its 650 illustrations was instrumental as well.

We walked on the road's shoulder in the direction of town afterward, damp, wearing wet shoes and singing choruses of "A hundred bottles of beer on the wall," until we saw the green station wagon explode through sunset and distance like a meteor.

Kooch's mom was flustered, embarrassed and likely relieved. She had forgotten us, she confessed, and apologized several times, but she didn't need to.

It was us who owed a debt of gratitude.

And we still do.

Bust Out The Copper Pot

I'm getting ready for the spring turkey season and this time, I'm really going.

It's been several years since I sat against a tree like in the movies, or the drawings in the sporting magazines. A gun teetering on a knee, its barrel pointing in the general direction of a decoy while a snivelly snowfall whitens the ground.

Not everyone does it this way, but I am going to.

There was an attorney I know who told me he was traveling to town when he spotted a gaggle of turkeys — a couple jacks, some hens and a tom — all fluffed and ugly-wattled in a gravel pit. The opportunity was too much for him. He stopped his car and gestured to his wife with a finger across his lips.

She was aghast of course and would have told him so, but they were on their way to dinner and a movie and the ambiance of the idea lingered in the air.

He climbed out, opened the trunk, removed a scattergun he kept there for occasions like this, before sneaking over the berm of the pit where the birds had gone. He shot the tom as it fanned its tail and dragged its wings, showing off, as it were, in an effort to make good with a hen.

The attorney carried the bird back to the car, placed it into the trunk and he and his wife continued to dinner feeling good, now that the turkey tag in his wallet had been notched.

Back then, you were allowed to harvest just one bird, and he had done it in a button-up shirt and Sunday shoes.

In those days, sportsmen pressed the Idaho game department to open the turkey hunt a few weeks earlier when the toms were gobbling. Biologists replied, toms gobble all year long.

Most hunters disagreed.

I learned later the biologists were right.

Aside from the savvy ascribed by Ben Franklin, and its portrait on the label of a bottle of bourbon I was still unfamiliar with the bird when I bought my first tag decades ago.

A guy at the Big Horn show, a Spokane Wash, grand meme that happens each spring drawing hunters, gear sellers and manufacturers from across the nation, laid out a simple formula for bagging a wiley Merriam turkey. This man was a self-described, unbelievably-astute buster of toms, and I sat for two hours through the same half hour lecture until I figured I had mastered this calculus that used mouth calls and a lot of camo.

I bought a mail-order cassette tape and a small box of calls to place on the back of my tongue and before long I could pipe along with a Charlie Daniels fiddle tune.

The next thing I knew I was up a river valley in the dark preparing to reconnoiter a quarry that was hyper astute, and highly sensitive to unnatural sounds that I wore sneakers to avoid being heard.

When I slammed the truck door, a tom gobbled back.

So much for the owl call — who cooks for you, who cooks for you all? — which the guy at the horn show marketed as a must-have.

I learned everyone kind of cooks for themselves in the turkey woods, and some birds come easily to a call while others won't.

It was a couple years later that one of my daughters, six or seven years old at the time, half-asleep, spring air reddening her cheeks and wisping her blond hair, leaned out the window of the pickup truck as we drove to school. She practiced on a gobble call she had fished from the glove box and called in two toms.

I slammed on the brakes.

The turkeys raced into the road from a greening hillside and strutted between potholes, their regalia fully rigged.

"Shoot it dad," another daughter, almost five at the time, whispered in awe. But, unlike the attorney, I left the blunderbuss at home, so we watched instead.

The tom I pummeled during my first spring hunt took several early mornings until I learned the formula: Turkeys leave a roost tree and follow a couple different routes to a food source where a bunch of birds gather. Toms are notoriously sidetracked by one hen or more.

Bang.

I admire people with the fortitude and patience to bag a tom with a bow, but I prefer the old-fashioned way.

Stealthily positioning for a tom to swing past a decoy just long enough for a hunter to hold tight, then squeeze, as the big bird glubs, its face glowing purple and his tail fanning like a Thanksgiving postcard, tickles me a bit.

It allows me to carry something out of the woods without breaking too much of a sweat.

Wear No Red Or Blue
And Let The Gobblers Come To You

Turkey hunting isn't a shoo-in, even if you think it is.

Wasn't it just a decade or two ago that you didn't know anything about it, while now, you kind of consider it old hat?

Remember back then, on a spring morning, as you headed up the gravel road, after getting coffee and gasoline, wanting to get an early jump on weekend chores, brushing, felling, planting trees, and you saw the feather in the dust just lying there like a quill inadvertently left behind after signing a road right-of-way agreement, or something.

You stopped the pickup truck. There was no traffic. The only sound came from the plywood mill across the river. Its steady clank and hum, distant, and the wind had not picked up.

It was March, after an easy winter, not a lot of snow, which had melted by then, at least down near town where you had pulled over and gotten out of the cab under a canopy of fir, a few scattered pines.

The air was alive with the aroma of wood, needles, duff and dust, still unstirred by truck traffic, or rural commuters. The call of thrushes, wrens, the exuberance of a robin up the hill, the whistling and chatter distant and close by near the ambling river was almost effervescent.

You walked the road behind your rig and bent to pick up the barred tail feather. It was broad and long, a handsome banded brown — like walnuts or pecans, and the shaft was a creamy white.

You spun the feather between your fingers. The morning sun had scaled the peaks of the Bitterroots to the east and showered the road where you stood with mottled shadows and patches of light that seemed to steam.

Turkey. You said to yourself. Merriam.

You had seen the birds over the past couple of years as they secretly ran across a road, skirted the edges of fields, slipped into deep grass near the seeps that trickled all year. You had heard a distant gobble once or twice that seemed so far off and elusive that giving chase was never part of the plan.

Now, you spun the feather in your fingers, held it like a pen, looked around at the mountain's gradual swoop toward the river, its small benches and openings and the sunlight on your arms felt warm as a flannel shirt. Below you, a hay pasture that annually gave up five tons per acre, its ditches brushed with thorn and crab apple, the whole swath buzzed with insects much of the time. Turkey heaven.

The next day you drove to Spokane to the Big Horn Show because the radio said a famous turkey caller was giving lessons and you sat through the seminar three times. Doled out cash for a cassette and a box of diaphragm calls, and practiced until the Panhandle turkey season rolled around in May.

By then you had practiced every day on the way to work, slipping a diaphragm call from its clear plastic container into your mouth, tasting the metal and canvas, feeling the latex like a rubber band with your tongue. You had for weeks plugged the cassette into the player under the dashboard and for hours meticulously rehearsed each call, from the putt putt to the clucks that started slow and ended fast, the yelps and purrs, the cackle and soft meow.

You had talked turkey with the men that came into the sporting goods store on Main Street in an effort to learn where exactly a guy should go to find a gobbler.

When you took the kids to daycare, you had them practicing too with a box call. They hung out the window of the truck expecting a slew of gobblers to come running, and then one day ... they did.

Three big toms came off a hill dappled with shooting star and arrowroot. The birds' purple heads and red wattles added even more color to the day. You and the kids watched in amazement, as the toms raced into the road where you stopped the pickup truck and turned off the key. They fanned their tails and dragged their wings.

One of your daughters looked at you and mouthed the word, Wow.

Keep calling, you whispered, and she did, sliding the

handle over the chalk, making it yelp, and then the birds slipped down the hill to the creek, and you were hooked.

Remember that?

The first bird you called was a jake after a snow shower, in a small clearcut that checked out your decoy then putted away. The next morning, you moved near a roosting tree and heard the birds come off, doing the cluck cluck that ended in a whirr of wings, one at a time and then the big tom putted to your decoy, straight from a Mayflower ad. He fanned big and dragged his wings, and you wanted to watch, but blasted him instead. Eureka!

You learned not to wear red in the turkey woods — doltish hunters may mistake you for a bird's wattle — and to not chase a gobble. Sit still instead and let the birds come to you.

Others learned it the hard way, while you learned from the scuttlebutt, of their mistake, to sit tight, with your back to a tree and your gun on your knees.

If you sneak into another hunter's call you may get a butt full of BBs or worse: That was the word.

Since their introduction to northern and central Idaho more than 40 years ago, Merriam turkey numbers have burgeoned, the number of birds a hunter can kill in a year has quadrupled and the season was lengthened with an earlier start.

Regardless, calling and killing a turkey isn't always easy and success is only ensured through preparation. Just like back then.

And two rules apply:

Don't wear red.
And let the birds come to you.

In The Turkey Woods

This is the short version.

We parked the car and walked through a dark woods to a place where we sat with our backs to trees and listened.

It rained.

After daylight we started to call.

Eventually we had three toms heading toward us. They picked up hens along the way and didn't come to the gun. It rained more. The toms were still talking back, hours later, but we were wet and went home.

It's not the whole story.

Turkey hunting, like most worthwhile endeavors, begins before dawn.

The pageantry of preparation, the observations, smells, sights and sounds of a spring morning far from town, this pleasant cornucopia makes the hunt memorable.

Most hunts are like this by virtue of how we absorb details. Those minute perceptions we gather even while walking through the forest dressed like camouflaged bull fighters. Or, while purposely traipsing, trying to not trip over limbs and fall, scattering our dignity and the contents of our pockets.

That has not happened to me, at least not in a while, but I understand it could.

It's foolish to be on hands and knees using the flashlight of a cell phone to find the striker for the slate call.

Considering this possibility, we step lightly as we walk.

There are other things.

The glow of fawn lilies in our path look like small stars, and we make a note to pluck one on the way back to the car, although in all likelihood we will come back by another route.

We step over shooting stars too, thin blankets of the dainty purple flowers that in the breaking dawn are delicate reminders of things ephemeral.

In cut dirt, black and upturned, are the running tracks of deer or elk that burst across the shallow topsoil this morning, or maybe last week. They glow.

All the limbs fallen from the trees seasons back, their needles shed and bark peeled away making them slick in the early rain, appear in the half light to be shed antlers. We know from experience that they are not antlers and walk past them.

Ducks paddle in a pond that is silver and reflects a mercurial sky. Their feeding calls sound like, "get back back back back back." Then a goose on the pond has caught our silhouettes and starts its long scolding. The chant is loud and raucous. It is picked up by other Canada geese whose ancestors have used the swamp forever on their way north, and we upbraid ourselves in hushed tones because the geese will surely alert any tom turkey of our presence and ambition to gun.

Somewhere across a meadow a coyote has watched us since we hit the trail along the field. It stands motionless and invisible. We don't know it's there and don't see it turn tail, so to speak. If we had seen it go, we may wonder to ourselves about the origin of the phrase, "turn tail," and when and where it was first uttered.

There's a lot of talking in one's head on a hunt.

Especially while walking to the woods in the dark, and sometimes while walking out.

When more light fills the forest, I stand up from the tree that I used as a backrest and go looking for another place because the first spot you choose in the faint forest light is often not the best one.

When I return I can barely make out my son sitting against a fir with gray bark, because of his camouflage clothing and face paint. He realizes this and raises a hand. This is me, not a tree.

His shotgun barrel pokes out and wiggles as he stands up.

I tell him about a heavily used elk trail where a herd must have cleared a bank as it tumbled into the canyon, or clawed its way out.

It's just over there, I say.

We converse in hunting voices which are the same ones used around a sleeping baby.

We find another spot, walk over to it. It isn't far away, but it has a better aspect and is closer to a gobbling tom. I knock limbs off small trees, clearing a field of fire. As soon as I cut from a box call, a tom gobbles back.

It's often difficult in the slanting Panhandle country to know how far away a tom turkey is by its gobble. Sometimes, though, a tom will fly across a canyon to meet a hen, or a box call.

Not far from where we sit, the lake can be seen through the trees. The yellow pine near an old homestead measure twice the hugging girth of a person's outstretched arms. Getting to town for the pioneers who built the place back then, must have been a bear.

Idahoans.

What can you say?

And that's just the first hour.

It's not yet 7 o'clock.

The Song Of The Jake

Jacobs brakes are used to slow the engine of a diesel tractor trailer loaded with logs, cattle, or shot rock fresh from a pit when the truck needs to be slowed without the air brakes.

Air is a precious commodity in the trucking industry. It can run out at harrowing times leaving a truck spinning its wheels.

Known as engine retarders, or just Jakes, the compression brakes were developed commercially in 1961 by Clessie Cummins of Jacobs Vehicle Systems, hence the name.

Jake brakes are used extensively in places like the Idaho backwoods, with its switchback roads and steep grades, where bunks filled with timber are hauled to the low country — instead of using a flume, which is outdated, or trucks with water-cooled brakes, also beyond resurrection, or any other brake system subject to fail under duress.

Jake brakes are solid.

They have your back.

For many truckers cresting a hill unforeseen, or anticipating a comfortable descent, the Jake is the pixie dust that keeps them safe.

A guy from Oregon who long hauled for a while as a young man, before he carried a hamburger belly and gruffed gray and whiskered on the steel seat of a D8, remembered coming down the Columbia River grade near Vantage. He was fully loaded with 80,000 pounds of industrial steel, close to the maximum and exceeding the speed limit when he found himself spiralling down the Columbia River incline. He hit the Jake, letting the slow, smooth sojourn coddle him graciously to safety over the long highway bridge before heading up the other side.

Jakes are like that.

They let you relax a little.

A friend of mine first explained to me the origins of the brake in the woods of a logging show we both worked. He was a rigging slinger who had tried his hand at driving truck — mechanicing on the fly, he called it — and learned about retarding systems from the greasy, duck-billed man who kept our equipment running.

"It's called a Jacobs brake," he said, and I took his word for it.

It's been years since I was in the jaybird seat behind the engine of a rig that had one. But I remember still flipping the switch, the other hand on the wheel as the loaded Kenworth growled its operatic bass down a cliff-hanger road, like a big cat being scratched.

In rural Idaho, Jake brakes are what's left of work, and even here, our cities are moving out of town.

For those who know their calming effect, it's hard to take seriously people who complain about the Jake.

I lived many years on a dusty back road where the logging on the hills behind my house kept the deer and elk in feed.

When the trucks came down from the standing timber in the black, early morning rain of October their Jakes rumbled through the wooded swales rousing me from my sleep. Just in time.

The song of the Jakes were preceded much earlier by the solemnic clanking of trailer chains lulling dreams as the trucks climbed the hill halfway between midnight and the bubble of the coffee maker.

Anyone who has worked in the timber industry — with its tattered clothes, wire rope, pumpkin patches, reprod and sawdust dreams — welcomes the song of the Jake.

It conjures the aroma of wood and floury road dust that squeaks under the soles of your boots.

It is the sound of industry, a tax base, money for schools and roads.

We don't talk like that much anymore, because we're almost through a quarter of the 21st century and income is mostly derived in a cloud.

The Jake brake, however, is still a part of the Idaho backwoods and back roads.

And truckers are glad for that.

The throaty bawl of a Jake drifting from a timbered valley in the morning is cemented in their psyches like baseball, a

40-yard drive to the red zone or a heavyweight match.

It's the solid handshake of the trucking industry, it's the ballcap when there's too much sun, and beer on ice after a day eating dust.

It's the box end wrench in the side pocket of their riggin' jeans.

And whether they prefer a Mack to a Kenworth, the driver's know that the Jake always has their backs.

Scents Of Spring

Skunks aren't cats.

They are named for them in some parts of the country, but they are distinctly different creatures.

There is nothing catty about a skunk. They lumber, toddle, sniff and raise their bushy tails like a peacock plume when frightened or simply upset. They do this in the dark, in spring — when the first robin flutes from a barely-budding aspen and collared doves pipe from the tip of a fir.

Early spring mornings are also the time when the guy delivering the newspaper careens around a corner in a minivan, not expecting to meet a jogger who didn't expect the nearby cat to be a skunk.

Unlike a cat, skunks take their sweet time snuffling garbage cans with their pointed noses and beady eyes and sometimes you don't see a skunk, just smell it.

The tangy aroma — an oily, pungent, eau de toilette that lingers and garners attention — can make a person survey their surroundings like on a quick mart camera. But it's night and the prevailing thought is, where's the skunk? Is it close enough to step on? Because that would be a pile of bad.

Skunks are better observed in daylight. In the event a skunk is struck by a newspaper carrier's minivan — its stout body feet up with Xs in its eyes — it can be safely poked with a stick, but be careful.

A pancake-like skunk on a highway might just as well be a cat, except for the smell, which is a sign of spring, just like the fluting robins and the calling doves and the sandhill cranes that fly over town in great flocks before daybreak, cackling in a chorus that makes you stop and crane your neck, but only briefly because, well, skunks.

Keep your eyes peeled.

When I was a kid, my neighbor called excitedly because he had caught a badger in a trap. Badgers were worth $7, he blubbered. Their hair is used for shaving brushes, the fur buyer had confided. I walked across fields, through strips of forest, and near a fence line overlooking a river we stood looking at his drag, which is a long thin cable tied to a trap that led down a hole in the dirt. We pulled it, and it pulled back.

What should we do? He asked.

I'll yank it out and you shoot it, I offered.

With each of my yanks, however, it pulled back more ferociously, and the more I considered it, the less confidence I had that my pal Robbie and his grandfather's bolt action .22 could stop the buzz-saw teeth of a mad badger on a leash.

I hiked home and days passed before Robbie returned to

school, the smudgy aroma of a polecat, not a badger at all, still seeping from his pores.

A biologist told me that skunks can't spray when their feet are off the ground. He smiled when he said it. He didn't smile a lot, so it concerned me. Try it, he said.

That was in the days before Siri, who has since advised that all animals are unpredictable.

Once a pal and I found a live skunk peering up from inside a steel 50-gallon drum sunk into the gravel alongside the railroad tracks where trains crossed a wooden bridge. We had been grouse hunting, a laborious process that required miles of treading along brushy fencerows and swamp edges, while keeping alive the lightning-quick reflexes that must be called upon if a grouse momentarily flared up, breaking hours of tedium. We used the tracks to walk home because we weren't old enough to drive. We came upon the skunk, looking rat-like and forlorn in 8 inches of water at the bottom of the barrel. We gathered sticks to build a ladder for the animal to climb out, but it only hissed menacingly and lifted its wet tail.

That's no way to go, my pal exclaimed.

Starving to death in a barrel?

He offered a coup de grace and carefully lowered the end of his 20-gauge grouse gun, slowly squeezing the trigger until the stock jumped in his arms and an eruption of skunk parts and perfume, oily railway water and a pile of debris spewed like a geyser from the opening.

He had just enough time to close his eyes.

Walking home behind me, his shirt and pants slowly drying

and the acrid fizzles of skunk parts in his hair, he blamed the lousy polecat for the mess he was in.

But it's spring. And skunks are part of the picture. They climb onto porches scavenging pet kibbles, they dig under decks and seek out refuge in garages and garden sheds from neighborhood dogs and cats that hamper their omnivorous discontent, all the while announcing their presence with what some refer to as an odious aroma.

But it's really not odious at all, it just smells like a skunk, and soon it will be replaced with blossoms, which emit a different kind of fragrance that is just another presage of winter's demise.

Spring Deer Sign

The scrapes ringed his property like casual provocations.

They weren't meant to egg him on. They were just the circular patches of earth, torn up by a whitetail buck's hooves to mark a place to communicate with other deer.

From his porch my neighbor could point them out along the edge of the young pine, fir and spruce trees that were his livelihood because this man raised trees for Christmas, and for residential landscapes.

He pointed to the places he knew the whitetail buck had pawed the ground and left its scent.

One over there, and across the road over there, and back behind the barn, he said. He counted them pointing with an arm outstretched, his other hand stuck in the pocket of his sagging jeans.

He knew where the scrapes were and that the whitetail buck that made them snuck around at night mostly, and only once or twice did he see the animal at dusk. When he walked out to check for sign, the buck had often been there.

Sometimes you don't find last autumn's buck scrapes until spring.

T.S. Eliot — the poet — called April cruel, but for most North Idahoans it's bliss compared to the months that came before.

The other day, as the morning sun warmed a glade and threatened to get hotter, I found a place where a buck had spent time last fall. I noticed the rubs where his antlers had peeled bark as sunlight crested a knoll, shining on the white fir scars thickened with pitch.

When I walked over, I found a scrape as big as a floor mat under a tree. Leonard Lee Rue, a man who spent a lot of time with whitetails and whose books teach anyone who wants to know about deer, measured hundreds of scrapes in the Eastern U.S. and found the majority to be patches of torn up dirt about 3 feet wide, several inches deep and always under a bush or tree with limbs hanging low enough for the buck to lick and hook his antlers.

North Idaho whitetail deer scrapes are about the same.

Elk are different. They churn up dirt and muck in a wooded seep and wallow in it, leaving a heavy scent.

Whitetails may urinate or defecate in a scrape, but they don't leave much behind that we can smell.

"I have carefully sniffed a number of scrapes, and the only odor was that of fresh earth," Lee Rue wrote in The Deer of North America.

Scrapes are often checked by residential deer and others

moving through the area. They each learn things about the buck that made the scrape, and the buck in turn learns things about visiting bucks, and does.

When you find a buck hangout in the spring, you wonder about the deer's size, where he dropped his antlers and if he's still alive. You wonder where he is, right then.

And you consider the best vantage to catch this deer next fall.

That's never easy.

Big bucks cruise a lot, and spotting one in daylight at a scrape is rare.

I sat on an overturned bucket once in the attic of our barn where the wide door, made to accommodate hay bales, was tied open with baling twine.

When the wind blew, the door bumped but quietly and the sound was common to the deer that passed through the area because I had tied the door years earlier.

I sat on the bucket waiting for a buck that had made a scrape across the meadow under young white pine at the edge of the field. I waited there for several hours each day for a week, and then he came, moving steadily like he was stuck in third gear, his antlers a heavy and symmetrical set of 4 or 5 points each. He cruised by the scrape, stopping briefly as I raised the .257 Roberts and its Bushnell 3x9. He was behind some fanning limbs, his back to me, then broadside, and then, his head and antlers tilted down, he disappeared.

And that was it.

It went that fast.

It was the middle of the rut and I knew that buck would check the scrape eventually, but I was surprised to see him. I had not accounted for my own complacency, the screen of limbs, the wind and the deer's own sense of survival.

He didn't need to wait around to learn if a doe, or another buck had checked his scrape. It was daylight. Vulnerability played a role. He had it figured out in 3 seconds, maybe 5.

If I had been given 10, I'm not sure I could have killed him.

Scrapes are like that.

They are supernatural in some ways because what a buck with its 300 or more scent receptors learn from them, and how quickly, we'll never know.

To walk a deer trail in the spring, ducking limbs, feeling rubs and checking scrapes, is an education.

It spurs imagination too.

And it's part of what keeps us going back to the woods.

Summer

SOMETIME, IDAHO

How It Is On The River

This man wore a wide brim hat like someone who might sell Cuban cigars, or at least be smoking one.

But he didn't deal in tobacco or appear to use it.

He stood in a turnout above the river, a spot he jockeyed his older model Datsun into a few seconds before I had the chance to occupy the space. An oncoming string of RVs on the river road that I hadn't expected at midweek, and pickup trucks towing trailers prevented me from turning.

He may have been a little gleeful to be the first to motor into the turnout. It accessed one of my favored fishing holes. And now he stood in the sunlight hurriedly piecing together a fly rod, running line through its eyes and tying on a leader.

I walked over.

"Can you stick that tag line through there?" he asked. "My eyes aren't what they used to be."

He was 80 years old. Looked it anyhow, which softened my demeanor.

"You fish this spot a lot?" I asked.

We were in a turnout that wasn't immediately noticed by most anglers who sought out the big, paved parking spots or ones distinguished by landmarks, beautiful bubbling runs, or road signs. This spot was partially hidden by elderberry and chokecherry bushes and the river wasn't visible from the cab of a passing vehicle.

"Ever since the road was put in," he said.

Which was before my time.

I pulled the tag end through the loop and he quickly placed the formed knot in his mouth to wet it, before pulling it tight with gnarled hands and the kind of thumb nails that doubled as screwdrivers. Then he tied on a big black ant.

"It's the only fly I use," he said.

That made it simple.

I inquired, but he assured me that he didn't need any help getting down to the river.

"I usually slide down on my butt," he said.

I hadn't seen him on these waters before and pried to check his familiarity. If you're at a place often enough you become intimate with cars and faces, and who camps where, and at what time.

"I come back here a lot," he said. "But anymore, it's usually in my sleep."

He chuckled. He wore a big shirt, shorts and river shoes and the back seat of his Datsun was sparsely occupied with fishing gear: some line spools, a second rod case and a few fly boxes. We spoke briefly about the river, the season and knots.

"I find that five wraps hold just as well as six," he said. "But sometimes I do seven."

He showed me his knot tying technique, a shortcut, and how he used a quick loop knot on the fly.

"Lets it wiggle," he said.

Pressing a pair of owl-like, wrap around sunglasses against his face, he said goodbye and slipped over the bank.

He had a fish on when I drove away realizing I had learned a lot in a few brief moments, from a complete stranger.

I didn't see him on the river again after that chance encounter in June. I would have noticed his small, beat up car with the Washington plates, straw plantation hat, and the short meticulous casts that distinguish some anglers from afar.

I looked for him.

I would like to say that's how it is on the river - you meet people whose company you enjoy - but mostly it's not.

Mostly anglers stay away from each other as they grouse about overcrowding or being corked by a guy in the kind of boat you seldom saw on the river years back. Other rivers had them, but not the ones up here, at least not after high water.

"Drift boats on the Joe?!" a barber in Sandpoint once exclaimed when I told him back then about a relatively new phenomenon.

"Getting more common," I said, and he looked out the window waywardly snipping his shears in the air.

More anglers from all over are acquainting themselves with Panhandle waters and midweek, once the best time for the therapy that angling can bring because the river was mostly isolated, can be just as busy as weekends.

It's easy to let the therapy sessions morph into a race for the next best hole, but it's also worth remembering that fly fishing isn't a full contact sport. And sometimes there are advantages to relaxing, getting to know someone new who shares a hobby with you.

I think a lot about the guy in the plantation hat. His ice blue eyes and liver spotted hands.

I wonder too at the things he could have taught given time, if I met him again on a bank, or knee deep.

Rivers are the perfect stage for picking stuff up and letting stuff go, for remembering and forgetting, and then recreating another version next season. They are also a place for embracing new things.

It's part of the flow.

That's how it is on the river.

A Sailor, His Sheepshank, Bowline And Hitches

I learned the sheepshank not because he tossed me a line and told me to tie one, testing me, like Quint in the shark movie; but because he instilled a desire to learn it.

From the first time I recall seeing Dick Eveleth wearing a beret on a day as overcast and foreboding as lead; to the last time years ago, under a curled Western hat, holding his wife, Jody's arm; there was always the hint of Texas in his voice, the flutter of a sail in his demeanor bucking a hard wind, and principle.

Between both times, 40-odd years had passed.

Dick Eveleth was a neighbor whose boat house was filled with projects, some of them going back to the days following the war, the Big One, when he had spent part of his time at Navy boot camp on the Farragut training grounds.

In his leaning boathouse — with its bats and rodents, its creaking timbers and oily rags — were remnants of engines from the 1950s. They were tuned and greased, their lower units sunk in buckets of water, their pistons briskly firing with one pull of the starter cord.

There were sailboats, catamarans, punts and dinghies in which his boys had learned the nuances and color of wind on water, how a gale dropped like an anchor from the top of an island and how to sail, or motor safely through swells too high for a prudent swain.

In the vintage boathouse — strapped to pulleys, wheels and rails, screwed to the rafters — hung tri-hulls, aluminum single hulls, cocktail class racers made of wood, pointed as the snout of a pike.

The eight-passenger family boat was stuffed in there too, with its hefty Evinrude Starflite, its red and white interior and electric shifter.

We were the work party in the spring that helped put the boats in the water and pull them out come fall, pressing each into the boathouse that leaned a little more every year, but is standing still despite almost a century of snow loads, storms and floods.

It was in the summer though that Dick and Jody — as we called them, always the two, always together — made their mark.

We often watched them come across the bay from a mile away, leeward before having to cut hard into the blowing spray, splashing off the hull until they glided into the flat water behind our peninsula and trolled to our dock.

We picked blueberries together, swam in remote parts of the lake, water skied, explored and worked. We painted cabins, cut cedar poles, built docks, moved rocks, tarred roofs and brushed trails. It was summer work and it was a good way for a kid to grow, and then Dick and Jody would have me in their sloop, Moondance, a boat Dick had salvaged, hearing another language.

With words like forestay, headstay, shroud and aft, Dick taught me port wine is red — an easy expression to learn that a boat's left side shows a red light at night, and he showed me bends and hitches, using the sheepshank to shorten a rigging line.

I was 4 or 5 the first time I remember seeing him. He brought over a freshly folded Stars and Stripes as a gift and asked my parents to put it on a pole and they did, on the lake side of the property, and Dick motored off into what looked like a storm coming.

Dick was a teacher most of his life, and twice a legislative candidate, believing every citizen had the duty to serve the country in some form.

When he died the other day at 90-something, I was sent a text message from across miles of water and wind, and storms somewhere brewing.

He hadn't been in a boat for a while, but I imagined his voice with the Texas in it, telling us to come about, as the sloop leaned hard, its heavy keel cutting the aqueous black under the hull, and the mainsail's boom swinging over our heads with sails fluttering before they caught wind.

He once undid a hitch I put on a cleat.

This way's better, he said. Look. And he re-tied it.

I spent hours afterward as a kid by myself learning to do it right, fast and by heart.

It was the principle of the thing, and Dick would appreciate it.

Boat Facts For The Faint Of Heart

There are some things you need to know about a boat and a lot of them happen in the back end.

This may not at first blush seem like much of a revelation, because the engine is back there after all, yet details must be addressed before the kick and sputter of the outboard.

The boat plug goes in the back. It prevents water from flooding the runabout.

Put it in before you go out.

Also, the back is where oily water sloshes around the transom from an outboard motor that drips petroleum products as it leaks and sputters. This filmy, tacky water that collects in the back must be sopped up with absorbent towels, or something from the Martha Stewart collection, if that's all you can find during a cursory search through a kitchen drawer. Sponges are good. Synthetic ones are best. Real sponges were once pulled from the bottom of the ocean along the coast of Greece by naked divers in row boats. They are no longer sustainable because it's not 1934 and the Aegean is being explored for its own petroleum potential. You can store fake sponges in a coffee can. Although real coffee cans aren't so easy to find as they once were, they are sustainable for the time being.

Boat sponges, it must be said, stay in the boat. They have been unalterably severed from their luxurious and glamorous beginnings in the bed and bath aisle of your local Perfume N' More the moment they are soaked in bilgewater mixed with Yamalube.

It should be noted also perhaps superfluously that the water coming over the stern as you back into a chop that pounds the dock like a steady drumbeat when the wind is right, and quickly fills the hull, is why you have a bilge pump. The bilge lies at the lowest point of the hull in the back of the boat like a gagging sailor hiccupping as it sends bilgewater back into the lake.

If there's too much water coming over too fast, your boat will sink.

If you have possession of a boat for a while — yours, or your neighbor's or a lucky, fish-chaser loaned by a friend — the ownership inherent in having this vessel under your feet as you power across miles of open water with a grin pasted to your face like cheddar burned to a frying pan requires you be a little afraid.

Fear is essential to all good boatmanship.

The floating fob fastened to the boat key, reminds you of this.

Sometimes the fob includes a chord that attaches to your

wrist or ankle in the event you are separated from the boat. This could occur if the vessel strikes a rock not shown in the chart you have meticulously pored over before casting off, or the floating logs we call dead heads, or if you perchance tip unbalanced overboard after striking a freakish wave.

Your falling out of the boat results in the key being pulled from the ignition, killing the engine.

It's so the boat doesn't aimlessly circle around you with a stainless steel prop chattering like shark teeth looking for some flesh to chew. Or, it ensures the vessel, unmanned, stops so you can swim to catch it.

All of that should induce fear, and it does.

The floating fob, usually a yellow PVC soft foam, also prevents the boat keys from sinking.

In some places sinking keys are fish food.

That sounds unusual, but I knew a man who claimed to have caught a 12-pound lake trout on a plastic Batman figure tied to a hook that he dropped over the side of his boat with a steel weight to make it sink.

Those macks will eat anything, he said.

I don't know about you, but the thought of losing the key of a borrowed boat over the gunwale in 50 feet of water makes my knees knock, even without the presence of fish.

They're knocking now.

That's how fearful I am of losing boat keys.

Once as a kid, my dad dropped the keys to our boat into Smart Bay, which immediately became a real dumb place to do that. We floated for hours that evening waiting for passing boaters to not just wave back, but to motor over and ask if we needed to be towed to the docks.

Moorage is another item on the checklist that must be considered by any earnest boatman.

Fishing is best when the wind is from the west, Izaak Walton wrote and I can attest he was correct part of the time. Fish bite the least when the wind is from the east. Another saying attributed to the father of fishing. Where I'm from, an easterly wind sends waves over the top of the dock and anyone who has tried to move by hand a boat that is being tossed in a semi-gale knows it is a difficult task requiring much sacrifice. Even in lesser spurts of weather, there's no time to fish when wrestling with a fiberglass Boston Whaler and its 75 horsepower motor when the wind wants to paste the ensemble to the shore.

Those are just a few things about boats to keep in mind when someone calls them pleasurecraft.

I know a person whose eyes automatically roll at the phrase.

She owns a canoe.

And she's never lost a trailer hitch, or had to backtrack 75 miles to return one.

Diving For Cash

Some days we dove from the boat in the late afternoon to frog swim deep into the murk until our ears popped.

From the depths we fished up a few cans that an adult, teetery with too much trolling, had dropped overboard earlier in the summer.

We knew where the cans were because my pal Honer and I had marked the spot just like Uncle Jim had taught, with something he called triangulation.

We used three points: a jagged rock on shore, a beacon down-lake on Gruben's Point, and across the narrows where the big pine leaned off the edge of Raspberry Island.

Close enough.

The lines crossed at the spot.

We cut the Johnson 18 and when the boat lost forward momentum, we dropped anchor, carefully bouncing it on the bottom, feeling for the edge where the slate turned to sand.

Fish-finders, back then, mostly showed depth and squiggly

shoals and rocks and structure on a screen the size of hard tack and were just about as useful. Mostly anglers relied on other things to find fish such as lake charts, experience or triangulation.

We took turns in the blue evening, slipping over the gunwales of the 14-foot Crestliner and swimming down past the small walleye that moved to shore from depths we couldn't fathom.

Even here, 15 feet under the lake's surface holding our breath, scouring the darkness for the flash of an aluminum can nestled on the lake's bottom, the pressure squeezed our heads and had us fighting to keep from bubbling to the surface like a 10-cent bobber.

Fishing for stray cans of soft drinks or Hamms, and sharing the one or two we found, was how we calmed the day.

Shivering, goose skin speckled our tanned, thin arms. We passed a can around, watched the sun drop and waited for the wind to dry our hair and chase the bugs away.

During those days, when we hadn't been hunting bass or pike, or walleye — usually in the heat around noon — we snorkeled the shoals of that northern lake for lures.

We were freshwater Jacques Cousteaus, Honer and me, with one pair of fins between us and a pair of leaky goggles, filling our tackle boxes with the plugs and spoons that once belonged to others.

Those were joyful moments.

The curses of anglers who broke off Heddon Super Spooks, Rapalas, or a Lucky 13s that wobbled like wounded minnows into an abyss of underwater boulders only to get hung up, turned into attaboys for us.

We held our breath, carefully unhooked the lures from rocks and carried them to the surface.

Draining the water from our diving mask and taking turns, we went down again.

A fisher's indignation at a brand new Rebel crawfish wedged in a crevasse and lost, was our delight.

The vexed rant when a Dardevle or Luhr Jensen, its price sticker left on for good luck, hooked a sunken log, had us grinning like cats.

We counted our savings, high-fived, tuned up Waylon on the radio and made a wake to another shoal marked by buoys that the county set each spring to tell us where to dive for cash.

For a couple summers we didn't spend a dime on spinners, spoons or plugs. With the money we saved, we bought new reels and rods instead.

Even now, when I see an angler break off, I make a note as I did decades earlier.

I asked my son if he marked it.

Waddya mean? He asks.

That's a $9 sinking minnow, I say. Those don't grow on trees.

Sometimes they get hooked on them, then break off and drown.

Mark it, and come back, I encourage. Bring your goggles and swim fins.

Or someone else will be diving for the cash that could have been yours.

SOMETIME, IDAHO

Have Caddis, Will Travel

The elk hair caddis epitomizes in many ways the American West.

A long time ago, when my oldest daughter was small enough to wonder at the moon, we lay in a tent in the high country above McCall and listened as wild animals surrounded us.

This was an eerie night sound of groveling, digging, very big-mammal like. As we lay listening to the noises growing louder and more intense, we imagined monstrous mountain beasts, fanged and saber clawed, harboring unknown intentions surrounding us.

For many minutes we were entranced by the alien and vigorous bedlam that occured in the austere dark of a high mountain night a few feet from the walls of our two-person pup tent.

We were consumed with alarm until I leapt from the two-man with a flashlight prepared for who-knows-what, to find a herd of mule deer bucks in velvet, perplexed enough to stop chomping grass and take note.

What the ...? They must have thought. "Hey Charlie, check out the mountain man in his underwear over here ..."

Their eyes glowed in the flashlight beam before they returned to hoofing, uprooting and munching.

A day earlier we had traveled up the two-track, past gigantic globes of gneiss, hobbled over outcrops and lumpy meadows through glades of yellow pine, replaced at higher elevations with shorter, thinner, much older pinon of sorts, in an effort to fish a lake I had found on a map.

The only imitation flies I brought were a handful of elk hair caddis because they were the only flies I knew to tie, and I would like to say the trout in the high mountain lakes slurped them like pudding, but they did not.

They were after very small midges squiggling below the surface film.

Without realizing this, I crept ever deeper in an effort to cast farther out. The darker it got that evening, the closer the absolutely glassine water's surface edged near the tip top of my chest waders until, giving up, I baby-stepped backward toward shore.

On the way down the mountain the next day though, in creeks that carved through meadows where I crept on hands and knees, the caddis imitation enticed the bevy of westslope cutthroat that feared my silhouette. I slithered close enough to the streams to make long casts over the summer grass, landing the high-floating bug in glassy currents where it was snatched by small, aggressive fish that flipped in my hand like gem-colored jumping beans.

I threw the trout back, not that it matters. Old timers, who knew the backcountry when it was water-cooled brakes on logging trucks, loved to trundle to higher elevations and catch dozens of those little fish and eat them around a campfire like hot dogs. The Idaho fish and game department put an end to this practice by closing the streams to catch-and-keep, because many of the state's pure strain westslope cutthroat trout lived in those rivulets.

An attorney in St. Maries who camped up Mica Creek in the St. Joe country each autumn for 50 years told how you couldn't catch small westslope cutties when the sun was out, but the overcast that followed a rain had them eating bugs, dimpling the water's surface like a breeze and that was the best time to hook them.

Al Troth, who invented the elk hair caddis and tied flies at his home across the street from the college in Dillon, Mont., spent nights in spring at the vise. He — and later, he and his son — fished in the morning, slept during the day and tied again through the night for the next day's fishing while watching old movies on a television set out back.

The former school teacher and longtime fishing guide valued the elk hair fly because it imitated a lot of other bugs and it floated high in the slick tailwater of his home river, the Beaverhead, where he spent a lot of time waist deep.

Not too far from Dillon is a hot spring whose bar and tavern has ancient elk heads looking down on the dining hall, and nearby at Wise River a tavern for years had an elk out back. It was raised up from a calf in a pole pen. Its shed antlers still hang from the ceiling.

Troth, who grew up in Pennsylvania before moving to the West, appreciated the availability of good fly tying material.

Elk seemed to be everywhere back then, in the hills, the mountain edges, even in a pen at a local bar, so he acquainted himself with the nuances of elk hair. Cow elk hair is shorter, thicker and darker than bull elk hair and because of its larger diameter, it's more buoyant, making a good piece of cow elk hair a fly tying staple.

I carried my own versions of Troth's elk hair caddis because they were easy to tie and fish dug them. A handful were packed with the No. 4 Orvis in a steel tube I bought at a yard sale in Missoula. I kept them rolled up in a tent packed into the trunk of a small car that could go almost anywhere, because almost anywhere is exactly the place that harbored the streams and lakes that held the small, dappled native trout.

Somewhere in all of this is a phrase, quite Western:

"Have caddis, will travel."

Why You Took The Boat To Town

On days like this we took the boat to town.

That meant watching out for sunken logs in the bay where the sawmill was, and slaloming through the buoys that led through the narrows.

If the water was low, the reefs cragged up from the sky-blue chop like the maw of prehistoric animals that could — with a tongue made of rocks — maliciously lick the bottom off your boat if you disregarded the navigational aids.

The reefs could chew and spit out your propellor or munch the lower unit off your motor.

Care was required.

You had just the one boat and motor after all. There would be no more.

The duo replaced the season tickets others had to a family fun park with mini golf and bumper cars. They replaced the big screens and handsets your pals used to chase cyber killers through cyber villages while sitting on a real-life couch with a plate of seemingly-cyber looking hot pockets that came wrapped in microwavable plastic.

The boat and motor replaced vacations, movies, and long drives to beaches in other states or countries that you had read existed, but nothing like them existed here.

The boat was a 14-foot Crestliner and the motor, a Johnson, 18 horsepower that you learned to keep clean and well sparked, the lower unit greased and lubricated, and the cowling latched tight.

These were your tools, and what kept you on the lake pounding across Big Bay to Grubens for gas and to hidden bays for the fish whose patterns you knew, while living off air most of the time, supplemented by PB and J, and the sun that darkened your skin and made your eyes squint.

You had a fishing rod, too. And an old tackle box filled with lures with names, crafted by marketers you knew in your sleep.

The spinners, plugs and spoons were painted to look like minnows or frogs, or mice, or frightened ducklings that you knew would one day entice a large, wolf-like fish to strike.

So, you made room for them in the tackle box even though their big, barbed trebles only hooked spare line, spools, sinker packets and other lures that fell from the trays into the well where you found them later, their hooks rusted.

But you took the boat into town anyhow, because your neighbor on the island across the bay had a Heddon with glass beads inside that made a tinkling sound as it weaved on the mirror-like water when the air was heavy, after the sun fell behind trees, and the bugs came out.

You needed one.

You needed that lure, absolutely, to wiggle-waggle over the reefs when the sky turned dark as a bruise, and the wind stopped and the water became polished aluminum.

That is when the big fish moved into the shallow reef beds and you could drift without power and without fear over the gnarly expanse of rocks and water while casting at each fin flash, or swirl.

So you measured your fuel with a stick stuck into the tank.

A lot of things didn't work like they should, and the gauge on the steel gasoline tank that rode between your legs, was among them.

The stick said there was fuel enough.

And you measured your cash.

Dollar bills, a few, and some change.

You weighed the necessity of the plug with the glass beads inside, counted calendar days before next payday from your job cutting the neighbors' grass.

Then made a decision.

You would fish the narrows on the way back from the hardware store with the Heddon lure grinning from one of the tackle box trays. You would slip behind the navigational aids, past the silent, rocky crags covered with the egg-like excrement of gulls and ducks, to the weedy bays and maybe walk a top-water plug among them.

Or, cast out if you could, far enough with a big popper that you had snugged up tight on your 8-pound test line before jerking it to make a sound like a cork removed from a bottle. If you did it right, it was the mating call of a frog, you surmised. Puh-loonk, puh-loonk.

If a bass struck, it would make you jump, and that was one of the reasons you used it, or any of the other lures in your box.

And if you were fortunate and found the Heddon lure with the glass beads packaged in a small, cardboard box hanging from a hook in the hardware store, you would check the knot twice, and feel the line for abrasion. You would cast the lure quietly along the weed edges or into holes and, puckering your entire demeanor, reel it back.

You could hear the beads inside make a tinkling sound. Certainly a bass would strike.

The water would boil, the surface would splash, the rod would pulse with energy as you stood on the casting deck on the bow of that boat, alone out there in that part of the lake where the big boats dared not go. Standing on the bow, your weight lifted the back of the boat just a little, and your rod pulsed as you reeled and let the drag whine and the fish, its tail bubbling the surface it fought to avoid, shook down, throttled this way and that way, before racing into the shadow under the keel.

You knew it.

You knew this would happen if you got the Heddon lure with the glass beads that made a tinkling sound.

At least you had imagined it as you motored across the lake, through the maze of navigational aids and into the channel, where your wake roiled and slackened in water the color of iron.

And that's why you took the boat to town.

Old School Travel Comfort

There was a time when Honer's dad made Winnebagos.
Anything built like a box on wheels, with cushioned comfort that could sleep six while driving in daylight across North Dakota was a Winnebago.

Others might refer to it as a kiss from heaven because Dakota by daylight is, well, you know, and there are 340 miles of plain, flat, nothing but sun, corn and clouds, if you're lucky.

The rest area benches only sleep one, but it doesn't take long for someone to report to the highway department tawdry miscreants who are unshaven, snoring on a bench and sporting the shifty demeanor of wayward travelers. That's when the highway officials show up with cookies, a map and hot coffee in a Styrofoam cup to send you on your way.

"Yore heading ta Fargo, y'say? Well then, keep going straight and you'll be there by supper."

At least that is what Honer's dad reported.

I didn't travel much across North Dakota as a kid. My

159

parents wouldn't have it. Their threshold for children fighting in a car had a three-hour limit and if North Dakota had been on the itinerary, we would have owned a Winnebago.

The rotund travel coaches came in different shapes and incarnations back then, and maybe still do, but the upholstery was a marvel and the dining area doubled as a jackknife sofa — or a bed in a pinch.

As kids who spent some time around other people's Winnebagos, we liked to sleep on the dirt outside under the colorful canopy that folded forward on two aluminum rods.

It was something we colorfully referred to as "sleeping under the stars," which made a lot of sense until it rained.

Summers, years later, as Winnebagos toddled into town from the interstate filled with families of people we kindly referred to as tourists, I often wondered if Honer's dad had a hand in buttoning the mellow yellow upholstery inside those motor coaches. I thought about him tacking the trim around the cabinetry as ash curled from the end of his Pall Mall like the black snakes we burned on the sidewalk on the Fourth of July.

Once at a campsite in Montana, where I stopped to change my boots to fish, I talked with a man who owned one of the rolling Taj Mahals. He likened his gas mileage to an M1 Abrams on a good day, but oh, the wealth of a shower after a hard afternoon in the hammock, he said.

The other day, I followed a convoy of Winnebagos over the Bitterroot Mountains heading east and read out loud the names stenciled on their metal sides.

They conjured images of marvelous, wild places that can be experienced while sipping a beverage from behind a screened window of the motor coach:

Grand Teton, Denali, Terra Wind, Mountain Air, Chaparral, Wildcat, Wildwood, Surveyor, Sierra.

That sort of thing.

As I passed them, I imagined inside were people playing cards, watching taped episodes of "Live! with Kelly and Michael," and frying bacon on the stainless steel Avion Cayo stovetop.

Honer's dad no longer busies himself with these, although he likely scrutinizes their lines with the critical eye of a retired craftsman.

As someone who still likes to sleep on dirt, I view the big wagons surreptitiously.

Their aerodynamic luxury could bring a lot to an elk camp, it's true. And they would, any of them, bridge the gap, quite comfortably, between us and what lies on the other side of North Dakota.

SOMETIME, IDAHO

Little River A Long Ways Down

There's a little river that everyone knows.

By everyone, I mean the people who like to walk several miles to hook a fish and let it go.

It's a river with a name that tells of the big river it spools into.

It used to be the haunt of a lot of steelhead, those red sided trout that tail their way to birthing streams in an annual pilgrimage that anglers refer to as a "run."

"Little steelies used to run up that river by the gobs," one fisher, who is an old fisher now, said as he reminisced about the days when, as a younger man, he and his pals often hiked back to the little river and hooked 20-inch trout with the fluency of auctioneers at an all-day steer sale.

There are a lot of paths to this river; many of them are shorter than the 10-mile trail that follows the rush of water through tall trees and along rock cliffs as the little river tumbles down to the big fishing holes.

You can reach the honey holes from almost any direction, on a variety of trails, some of them entail casual hikes on well-worn paths that lead from parking lots with vaulted toilets, while others are bushwack trails and some require a good mule.

A lot of people, for many years have scouted the most reasonable access points to the best fishing holes, and once years ago, a man assured me he had located the nirvana trail that dropped quickly from the side of a mountain to one of the best fishing spots on the river.

"It is a half mile down," he said. "And 10 miles up."

In Idaho, there are still a lot of rivers like this one.

It is mythical, in a sense, because of all the tales told of its legendary cutthroat and bull trout.

And because of all the anglers who are aging now, or gone, who have for almost a century slipped along its boulders and placed dry flies where the water bounced and flattened in the summer sun.

The stories go back to a time when anglers delicately cast dries with bamboo fly rods, and later steel, fiberglass and graphite.

It didn't matter how careful the cast because the fish were always willing and the stories always engaging, and it's because of their relevance that the name of the river isn't mentioned.

Go there once, though, and you're hooked on it for a long time. Hike in any way you can, and exert the effort to reach its water and you'll find the solace of silence, mostly, without the growing tide of humanity that shadows the banks of many other rivers.

Stay for a day, and the river seethes its way into your system.

It remains there for weeks as you plot how best to proceed when again you visit.

What is the most optimal shortcut from a nearby peak, or ridge, or point of land?

What's the best route to find the most seldom-fished water?

At night the sound of the stream nudges you to sleep.

During the day you remember the behemoth cedars on the opposite bank and how the devil's club beneath them grew like wait-a-minute vines and scratched your legs as you slipped by eyeing the next wash, the next hole, the next run.

It's hard to shake.

I stopped along a gravel road one early morning this summer to talk with a fly fisher who, despite being hard at work on his job, was thinking of a good trout stream.

We pondered Panhandle rivers and how many are stocked with anglers riding float tubes or rafts, or just people relaxing on float tubes or rafts. Flotillas of them.

He lowered his voice and mentioned this small stream as if it was a blessing, a place only for people who relished its import.

"Have you been there lately?" he asked.

I had not been there in years.

But, his voice did it, as well as the watery, reeled-in look in his eyes when he mentioned the place.

"You've got to go this summer," he whispered.

From the Missouri River to the coast, a lot of fine fishing water plunges east and west, some is solitary and remote, some is a circus of Filson hats and Patagonia poster apparel.

This river is neither.

There's a story at every turn of this river. A tale in every canyon. The stories get bigger as the river widens and the holes get deeper and longer.

Just listen.

There is plenty of time to hear the tales on the long walk through the fir and pine-scented forest that engulfs it.

I'm going back, I'm pretty certain.

I have a map a man made for me on a piece of cardboard that he laid on the hood of his pickup truck to show the preeminent path to the most astonishing holes.

I'm going back to fish it, and to listen.

Maybe this week.